R. E. M.
BEHIND THE MASK

R. E. M.
BEHIND THE MASK

JIM GREER

·

PHOTOGRAPHS BY
LAURA LEVINE

Little, Brown and Company
BOSTON NEW YORK TORONTO LONDON

Copyright © 1992 by Joshua Morris Publishing, Inc.

First Paperback Edition

A Wilton House Book

Library of Congress Cataloging-in-Publication Data
Greer, Jim.
 R.E.M. : behind the mask/by Jim Greer; photographs by Laura
Levine.—1st American ed.
 p. cm.
ISBN 0-316-32730-1 (hc)   0-316-32732-8 (pb)
1. R.E.M. (Musical group) 2. Rock musicians—United States—
Biography. I. Levine, Laura. II. Title. III. Title: R.e.m.
ML421.R227 1992
782.42166'092'2—dc20   92-1767

10   9   8   7   6   5   4   3

RRD—OH

*Published simultaneously in Canada
by Little, Brown & Company (Canada) Limited*

Printed in the United States of America

This book is for Kim.

CONTENTS

PICTURE CREDITS

Joshua Morris Publishing, Inc., would like to thank the following companies and individuals for supplying photographs and memorabilia for this book.

PRELIMINARY

Facing contents page: Anton Corbijn
Contents page: (top left) Steve Double/Retna; (top right) Derek Ridgers/London Features International Ltd; (bottom right) A. J. Barratt/Retna; (bottom left) Tim Hall/Redferns

CHAPTER ONE

p. 11: Laura Levine; p. 12: Todd Ploharski; p. 13: Andy Catlin/London Features; p. 14: Todd Ploharski; p. 15: Laura Levine; p. 16: Todd Ploharski; p. 17: Laura Levine; p. 18: Todd Ploharski; p. 20: Laura Levine; p. 21: Laura Levine; p. 22: Laura Levine; p. 23: Laura Levine; pp. 24-25: Laura Levine; p. 26: Todd Ploharski; p. 27: Laura Levine; p. 28: Laura Levine; p. 29: Laura Levine; p. 30: Laura Levine; p. 31: Todd Ploharski; pp. 32-33: Laura Levine; p. 34: Laura Levine; p. 35: Laura Levine; p. 36: Laura Levine

CHAPTER TWO

p. 39: A. J. Barratt/Retna; p. 40: Todd Ploharski; p. 41: Peter Anderson/S. I. N.; p. 42: Todd Ploharski; p. 43: Todd Ploharski; p. 44: Todd Ploharski; p. 45: Laura Levine; p. 46: Todd Ploharski; p. 47: Laura Levine; p. 48: Todd Ploharski; p. 49: Larry Busacca/Retna; p. 50: Todd Ploharski; p. 51: Laura Levine; p. 52: Laura Levine; p. 54: Laura Levine; p. 55: Laura Levine; p. 56: Todd Ploharski; p. 57: Laura Levine; p. 58: Todd Ploharski; p. 59: Derek Ridgers/London Features

CHAPTER THREE

p. 61: Steve Double/Retna; p. 62: Todd Ploharski; p. 63: Steve Double/Retna; p. 64: Todd Ploharski; p. 65: Steve Double/Retna; p. 66: Todd Ploharski; p. 67: Larry Busacca/Retna; p. 68: Todd Ploharski; p. 69: Leo Regan/S. I. N.; p. 70: Todd Ploharski; p. 71: Michel Linssen/Redferns; p. 72: Todd Ploharski; p. 73: Larry Busacca/Retna; p. 74: Todd Ploharski; p. 75: Todd Ploharski; p. 76: (top) Michel Linssen/Redferns, (bottom) Todd Ploharski

CHAPTER FOUR

p. 79: Derek Ridgers/London Features; p. 80: Eddie Malluk/Retna; p. 81: Steve Double/Retna; p. 82: Michel Linssen/Redferns; p. 83: Gary Gershoff/Retna; p. 84: Tim Hall/Redferns; p. 85: L. Lawry/London Features; p. 86: Todd Ploharski; p. 87: Derek Ridgers/London Features; pp. 88-89: Youri Lenquette/Stills/Retna; p. 90: Todd Ploharski; p. 91: A. J. Barratt/Retna; p. 93: Derek Ridgers/London Features; p. 94: Michel Linssen/Redferns; p. 95: Michel Linssen/Redferns

CHAPTER FIVE

p. 97: Tim Hall/Redferns; p. 98: Kevin Mazur; p. 99: Youri Lenquette/Stills/Retna; p. 100: Dennis Keeley; p. 101: Anton Corbijn; p. 102: Frank W. Ockenfels 3; p. 103: Anton Corbijn; p. 104: Dennis Keeley; p. 105: Anton Corbijn; pp. 106-7: Kevin Mazur; p. 108: Kevin Mazur; p. 109: Kevin Mazur; p. 110: Dennis Keeley; p. 111: Anton Corbijn; p. 112: Johnny Olsen/Retna

CHAPTER SIX

p. 115: Eddie Malluk; p. 117: Todd Ploharski; pp. 118-9: Todd Ploharski; p. 121: Martin Benjamin/Retna; p. 125: Johnny Olsen/Retna; pp. 126-7: A. J. Barratt; p. 131: Michel Linssen/Redferns; p. 133: Ronnie Randall/Retna; p. 135: Michel Linssen/Redferns

ACKNOWLEDGMENTS

"I don't know why anyone would want to write a book about us," Michael Stipe said to me, after I mentioned that I'd agreed to do *Behind the Mask*. "We're so boring. Don't you know? All rock stars are boring."

I tried to explain that my book wouldn't be about his band so much as his music. Too much of the overample critical verbiage devoted to R.E.M. talks nonsense about the "mystery" enshrouding both the band and its music, especially the lyrics. My attempt here has been not to penetrate that mystery but to show that there never was any in the first place. It'd be hard to find four more forthright fellows in any field of endeavor; and their workmanship, in hard light and sharp focus, is equally direct.

In many ways, this is a queer little book, part history, part critical reassessment. It jumps around almost desultorily and nearly falls asleep in places, but always, I hope, with good reason. I spent a lot of time on early history because it helps define the band, and a fair amount on current events because it helps define where they're headed. I didn't spend a whole lot of time on the medieval period because I think the albums from those years tell as much of the story as needs be told (more or less). The critical views expressed are doubtless idiosyncratic, even sometimes whimsical, out of both conviction and a deep desire not to treat my subject with the reverence it too often is met with, and almost never requires.

I left things out, on purpose. Apologies in advance to all slighted egos. I made stuff up, too, on purpose (for instance: contrary to Chapter Two, none of Michael Stipe's lyrics are about his cats. He doesn't keep cats. Some of them, however, are about his dogs), but only as a (painfully obvious) joke and always to prove a point. I wrote very little about the personal lives of the band members, because that wasn't the point. Music doesn't need biography for relevance. Its impact depends more on the personality of the fan than that of the musician.

The result is my R.E.M., the one I've rearranged from the available materials. There are as many potential R.E.M.s as there are potential listeners, which, as you might guess, is a lot. If this book gives them another angle of perception from which to examine their fave rock combo, it will have done its job.

Thanks are due a lot of folks, without whom this book would have been, in varying degrees, a lot more difficult or less fun. To Mr. and Mrs. J. Bradford Greer, for their patience and understanding through the years. To Terry Monaighan for the idea and for seeing the book through. To Amy C. King and Melody Cassen for art direction and production. To Richard Gehr, for the reference. To Michael Pietsch, for the advice. To Daniel Fidler, for the research and "other" assistance, beyond the call of duty. To Mark Blackwell, for the original Athens trip. To Johan Kugelberg, for the encouragement. To Brooke Johnson, in R.E.M.'s office, for the unflaggingly cheerful help. To Susan DeCapite, for not always telling people where I was. To Lauren, Steven, Jonathan, Michael P., Alec, Staci, Mark W., Mark E., Nathaniel, Celia, and everyone (not necessarily still) at *Spin* for being so goshdarn cool. To Bob Guccione, Jr., for the chance. To Michael, Peter, Mike, Bill, Jefferson, and Bertis, for the love and understanding, or at least tolerance. To Paul Butchart, for the expert tour and mausoleum relics (and the comfy couch). To Kurt Wood, for same. To Steve Karas and David Millman at I.R.S., for the generous support.

To Todd Ploharski, for the invaluable, uh, stuff that would take too long to list here. Todd is among the foremost collectors of R.E.M. relics in the known universe. If you're interested in buying or trading same, get in touch with him at (404) 475-2204 or write 335 Ankonian Way, Alpharetta, Georgia, 30202. A lot of whatever's good about this book comes from him.

Some of the quotes in this book come from an interview I published (cowritten with Mark Blackwell) in *Spin* magazine in March 1991. Used with kind permission. The rest, with minor exceptions (noted in text), comes from original interviews.

C H A P T E R   1

A T H E N S , G E O R G I A
1 9 8 0 – 1 9 8 1

ATHENS, GEORGIA

B E H I N D · T H E · M A S K

The church on Oconee Street—where Peter Buck and Michael Stipe lived and later the whole band lived together (briefly); the impossibly dilapidated slum (rotting floorboards, torn-up "furniture," relentless beer-stench) where "only college kids could be convinced to live," according to Peter; the church where R.E.M. played its first show, on April 5, 1980, at a birthday party for friend and roommate Kathleen O'Brien (she organized it herself)—no longer exists. It's a parking lot now, although in a corner of the lot stands what looks like the burnt-out relic of a Dresden fire bombing and is, in fact, the stump of the steeple. Across the street, an empty lot covered in equal parts kudzu and trash marks where the "Jesus Saves"

house once stood (home of several Athens scenesters—so named because of the neon "Jesus Saves" sign buzzing nightly on the corner of the property), and adjacent to that is yet another vacant, rubble-strewn space, where Rick the Printer had his print shop, the same Rick the Printer who ran the 11:11 Klub on Clayton Street (doors opened at guess what time) where R.E.M. played its second

(free) gig, an occasion recorded for posterity by the Athens police, who busted the illegal club in response to a noise complaint in the small hours of the morning and took pictures of some of the offending clubgoers.

It's unlikely that the current residents of the brand-spanking-new condos erected near this

nexus have any clue to its history. If they did, they'd probably freak—R.E.M. is, to this day, the single biggest tourist attraction in town, and the number one reason many students decide to attend the University of Georgia here. The scene in Athens has changed considerably since the heady days of the late '70s and early '80s, although most of the changes are barely perceptible to the casual observer. And the bulk of that change is due to R.E.M., or more precisely R.E.M.'s success.

Athens is a relatively quiet town not far from Atlanta with about 70,000 inhabitants, 20,000 of whom are perpetually in transition from boys to

Above: Mike Mills, bassist profundo, in the spotlight.

Right: "It wasn't like this huge urge to be stars," recalls Peter Buck. "It just seemed like everyone else was doing it. It seemed like a lot of fun. And music was what we liked."

12

men and girls to women at the University of Georgia. Some never quite make the leap and instead form rock'n'roll bands; it's with these malfeasants that this book is concerned.

Like all relentlessly collegiate towns, Athens houses its share of shy, sensitive, misunderstood poets in thrift-store rags—girls and boys of such incomprehensibly bohemian ways that sensible frat boys go out of their way to hurl abuse and cups of stale beer in their direction. (Which, when you think about it, is sort of like feeding stray cats; it only encourages their alienation.) These waifs are both harmless and penniless, and will never amount to anything, which is why R.E.M. is just all wrong—these guys were boho college boys who made good, and boho college boys are never ever supposed to make good. No wonder every forward step in R.E.M.'s career has been met with renewed disgust and tortured, accusatory cries of sellout. Gentle souls claim singer-seer Michael Stipe as one of their own, and every move he makes to broaden the appeal of his message, however dripping that message might be with fresh coats of unfiltered aesthetic, is to them

a knife in the back.

This is the real R.E.M. enigma: not what Michael's really like (he's like you, more or less, except richer); or what the lyrics mean (most of 'em are easy to figure, the rest is just personal or universal "poetry"); and it's certainly not how they got to be successful (they worked really, really hard—good idea, my friends!). No, the real enigma is why the band was ever misperceived as "elusive" in the first place. Its members were never any different from the billions of arty college kids milling around every other campus, the same kids who made up the band's first audience and continue to constitute a significant segment of it. R.E.M. was just on a different side of the mirror.

Knowing that, it's easy to sense a certain ambiguity on the part of the R.E.M. boys toward their hard-won fame and fortune, a sort of uneasiness at what they still seem to consider their good luck in the face of some of their friends' misfortune. They've all four remained committed to the town that oversaw and supported their first fumbling efforts, investing money in restoring historic old buildings, participating in local politics, employing as many of their old friends as they can. Partly that's an extension of the fact that all four are genuinely nice human beings who feel uncomfortable being heaped with praise and outsize checks for just being "four shlubs who bang out some chords," as Peter Buck puts it. But a good part of it is pure and simple guilt—the R.E.M. boys are guilty of becoming rock stars. And that was never the idea.

The Athens music scene didn't start with R.É.M., by any means—in fact, some would argue, it ended with them. Its genesis was, really, in the mid- to late-'70s Athens art scene, which was fueled in part by the punk (and later new wave) explosion, both in London and in New York. Punk gave to the young and the art-damaged of Athens a freedom from the shackles of technique—meaning that the ability to play an instrument was no longer a requirement for starting a band. But in 1976 and 1977, few in Athens, or even in nearby cosmopolitan Atlanta, had heard of bands such as the Ramones, Talking Heads, the Sex Pistols, and the Clash, and those few who

---

Above: R.E.M.'s early success was predicated, above all, on the band's appetite for the road. Constant touring — at a time when there was no established club network for underground bands — brought rapid notoriety.

Right: Peter Buck: "Once you start playing out of town, it seems a whole lot better than working."

had were too far between to constitute any sort of scene.

One exception to that rule was an Atlanta-based group, the Fans, which drew its inspiration partly from the punk ethos but which nevertheless was very explicitly non-punk in execution (i.e., the band could actually play). The Fans had been around, in any case, since 1975, garnering critical acclaim for their early-Roxy Music-derived art rock, but little popular support. These qualities were what made them cool to then-Atlantan record store employee Peter Buck, who claims that if not for the Fans there would never have been an R.E.M.—meaning that it was their example that, helped inspire him in the first place to want to start a band.

Buck was born in Los Angeles but spent most of his formative years in San Francisco and later in Indiana, before his family moved to Georgia. An abortive stint at Emory University and an attack of romantic wastrelism behind him, he found a job at a record store called Wuxtry's in Atlanta in 1977. In December of that year, he helped arrange a party at which the B-52's played and was impressed enough by the band and by the crowd of Athenians it had brought in tow that when offered a job at the Athens Wuxtry, Peter jumped at it.

Once in Athens, working at the record store

proved an ideal way to meet the movers and shakers of the embryonic music scene, including a shy young art student who would often come into the shop with two cute girls, looking for obscure 12-inch singles. His name was Michael Stipe, and the two girls weren't his girlfriends (as an impressed Buck originally thought) but his sisters, Lynda and Cyndy. Eventually, Peter and Michael became roommates out at the church on Oconee Street where Peter had been given the lease by his boss at work. As the two would sit around watching junk television, listening to records, and drinking beer after beer, they slowly began to think about starting a band. After all, it seemed, all their friends were doing it. And where Peter's lack of technical competence on the guitar had always in the past deterred him from pursuing the rock band thing, the example of the B-52's—right in his own backyard, as it were—had showed him that his level of proficiency mattered not one whit.

Catalysts not just for Peter Buck but for the

Above: The early Athens scene centered around Tyrones — R.E.M. was the first so-called New Wave band to bring capacity crowds into the club.

Right: "Our goals were a little different [from most Athens bands]," recalls Peter. "One great single — that's what we wanted."

whole Athens scene, the B-52's formed in late 1976 and played their first gig on Valentine's Day, 1977, in a tiny alcove of the living room of one of the more notorious party houses in Athens, across from the Taco Stand ("T-Stand" to locals) on Milledge Street. At that first performance, and for several ensuing ones, the band didn't even have a drummer, but played to taped accompaniment. As the B-52's grew more serious in intent, they set up a rehearsal space in the bloodletting room of a mortuary downtown, an extremely nonspacious environment with slanted floors leading to a gutter which is still stained brown from the blood.

After the band played a few dates in New York at Max's Kansas City, and at a "punk festival" in Atlanta, local Athenian Danny Beard offered to finance a single on his newly formed DB Records, which the band duly recorded and released in May 1978. The record was "Rock Lobster" b/w "52 Girls," and it was an almost instant success, selling an eventual 17,000 copies—phenomenal for an entirely independent label—and prompting several major-label offers. In April 1979, the B-52's signed to Warner Brothers and soon thereafter moved out of Athens for good, leaving behind them, instead of a disorganized, unfocused bohemian party circuit, the beginnings of a formal music scene.

"What happened to the B's," recalls Peter Buck, "was just so out there. It was just like if you had a best friend who was killed by a meteor: You wouldn't worry about going out of the house, 'cause you wouldn't worry about getting hit by a meteor. Everyone just assumes, Well, that's once.

It was like, now you know someone who's in a band, and has a record contract, but it ain't gonna happen again."

Nevertheless the impetus of the B-52's success, however astounding it must have seemed, played a major role in the ensuing influx of arty bands in town. In rapid succession, the Tone Tones, Pylon, the Method Actors, and several others formed from either friends of the B-52's or kids who'd been inspired by them. The entire "scene" in town at this point consisted of probably 100 people, all of whom knew each other. At first, there was nowhere for the new bands to play except in each others' basements, at parties, which suited them just fine—few held careerist motives in those heady, alcohol-drenched days. The B-52's had been, first and foremost, a transcendent party band, and that was a fine enough goal for Athens's finest.

Then the local club Tyrone's, formerly not known for its adventurous booking policy, booked the Tone Tones for a normally slow Tuesday night and were surprised at the hopping art crowd the band drew. Soon after, Pylon played and drew even more people, establishing a regular new wave night at Tyrone's, toward which the scene naturally gravitated. Unfortunately the art kids spent almost all their time on the dance floor and very little at the bar, which, combined with the fact that few of them had money to spare on beer anyway, did not endear the crowd to the proprietors of Tyrone's.

A rare videotape of a Side Effects gig in 1981 at Tyrone's gives a good indication of the way things were: A less-than-capacity crowd makes up in enthusiasm what it lacks in body count, whirling, shaking, and bopping with heedless abandon to the tight dance rhythms provided by the band, which seems to be enjoying itself at least as much as the crowd is. A far cry from the atmosphere at almost any college-rock concert in any town today, where the patrons stand stolidly as if enduring some grave punishment, regardless if the music being played is unadulterated genius or (more likely) mediocre art pap.

A corollary to the developments at Tyrone's was the creation of the legendary 40 Watt Club. Taking its name from the loft parties Pylon's Curtis Crowe once threw in a small, poorly lit space on College Avenue, the 40 Watt East, across the street on the corner of College and Broad, was either the first or the second of six or seven incarnations of the club, depending on if you count Curtis's loft. It opened on May 20, 1980 (the Side Effects played), and quickly gained preeminence among the art kids as a weekend night spot (it was only open Fridays and Saturdays, and some Thursdays, but Tyrone's hardly ever had a new wave band on the weekends anyway). On nights when bands would play, the floors would shake so hard from dancing that owner Paul Scales would have to run downstairs to the sandwich shop and brace the ceiling with timber. From the street outside, you could actually see the windows bulging out from the pressure inside. On a typical summer night, especially one when R.E.M. was playing (on nights when they weren't you could often find either Peter Buck or Michael Stipe serving drinks behind the bar), the temperature inside could get well above 100 degrees.

John Michael Stipe was a well-traveled army brat by the time he arrived, ostensibly to study art (especially photography), in Athens. Although born in Georgia, he'd spent so much of his childhood being uprooted (his family spent time in Texas, Germany, and Illinois, too) that he felt very little like a native when they moved back in 1978, in Michael's 18th year. A moody, word-struck young geek—by his own account, a painfully shy individual whose best friends were his sisters—Stipe nevertheless struck up a friendship with the outgoing Peter Buck in the course of his frequent visits to the Wuxtry.

Above: R.E.M.'s do-it-yourself ethic, derived from the similar attitude of punk rock heroes like the Damned and the Buzzcocks, was reflected in their deliberately low-tech posters.

THEY CAME, THEY PLAYED, THEY BROKE UP:
A RUNDOWN OF THE IMPORTANT ATHENS BANDS PRIOR TO AND CONCURRENT WITH R.E.M.

THE TONE TONES

Athens's second band was started by transplanted Atlantan Nicky Giannaris, who was inspired to move to Athens after seeing the B-52's at the Atlanta Punk Festival; the band's first gig was opening for the B-52's at the Georgia Theater. Vic Varney and David Gamble, later members of Method Actors, were also in the band, which broke up shortly thereafter, in true art-school fashion, due to creative differences among the members.

PYLON

Athens's second *popular* band, Pylon followed the B-52's blueprint of playing a few shows in New York to create a critical buzz and releasing a single on Danny Beard's DB label. The band consisted of Michael Lachowski, Randy Bewley, Curtis Crowe (whose loft was the original 40 Watt Club), and singer Vanessa Ellison. Pylon played sharp, lean, untutored, but tuneful songs that provided the band with a good deal of critical attention but limited commercial success, in part because the band wasn't a tour hound like R.E.M. Pylon would break up a number of times, reforming as recently as 1990 (and breaking up again soon thereafter).

METHOD ACTORS

Vic Varney and David Gamble, after the breakup of the Tone Tones, decided to carry on as a guitar-drums duo—the theory being that with fewer people there would be fewer disagreements. Their dissonant minimalism ensured them a limited audience, although the pair did end up a fairly large European cult item, completing a number of successful tours on the other side of the pond.

LOVE TRACTOR

Formed in June 1980, by Mark Cline, Mike Richmond, and Kit Swartz (also in the Side Effects). An all-instrumental band, at first, Love Tractor described its music as "existential Ventures meets the Cure." Armistead Wellford later joined on bass, and Bill Berry played drums for a while, before deciding that R.E.M. was the band he loved. Actually a difficult choice at the time, although in retrospect probably the correct one.

SIDE EFFECTS

Paul Butchart, Kit Swartz, and Jimmy Ellison's band debuted the same night as R.E.M. The Side Effects played what they called "bomp and stomp" music: vigorously rhythmic, but less serious and arty than Pylon. The Side Effects were an art-school party band, and the ecstatic, Dionysian revels attendant upon their performances were an integral part of what insiders will forever consider the "real" Athens scene (which ended when careerist bands started moving to town because it was the hip place to be). Once the scene changed, the dancing stopped, and with it a large part of the initial impetus.

OH OK

Linda Hopper, Lynda Stipe (Michael's sister), and David Pierce. Like most Athens bands, Oh OK was formed by people who'd never been in bands before and couldn't really play instruments. What Oh OK had going for it was a seemingly genuine childlike quality that proved a marked contrast to the almost cynical, self-conscious näiveté of some of the other bands. Oh OK was to be one of the last noncareerist Athens bands.

Of all the members of R.E.M., Stipe has always been the one most interested in visual arts—if not the only one interested—but his artistic bent has always propelled him in several directions at once. Both before and after the band, he was involved in a number of low-key, earnest art "projects," which seemed, more than anything else, the result of an uncontrollable urge to create or even beyond that—to produce. Stipe has always been monu-

mentally productive: Even after R.E.M. started, he found time to participate to some degree in at least four other musical ventures. His interests weren't limited to music, either: He put together issues of a little photocopied art-zine he called Momo and sold for a quarter each to whoever could spare the change (not many could in those days, and existing issues—I've seen two different ones—are few). He also contributed to a local fanzine called *Hot Java*.

Stipe's obstinate productivity is one of the main motors that drives R.E.M. Even today, his creativity can't be contained within the confines of the band; and where Peter Buck's equally daunting work ethic is focused almost exclusively on music, Stipe's catholic reach extends to films, video, painting, photography, folk art, poetry, and politics, in addition to his extra-R.E.M. musical projects. The comprehensive nature of Michael's interests and accomplishments bespeaks not only a restless intelligence but a restless nature as well, possibly derived from the changeable life he became accustomed to as a kid.

Bill Berry and Mike Mills, friends from high school in Macon, Georgia, started out not being able to stand the sight of one another and ended up best friends—just like in the movies. Bill was the wild one, the bad kid, the one who drank beer and skipped school and beat up kids like Mike Mills, who didn't touch drugs and got really good grades and looked the part.

When Bill showed up one day after school at an impromptu jam, he discovered that the bass player was none other than Mills, whom he despised, and almost walked out. Bill decided to stay and the

pair became fast friends and an even faster rhythm section. They played in all sorts of lame cover bands until deciding one drunken night to enroll in the University of Georgia, where they arrived in January 1979. With their instruments.

Bill's girlfriend Kathleen O'Brien, who lived in the church with Peter and Michael, is the person technically responsible for bringing the members of R.E.M. together (although Athens is such a small town the four would inevitably have come to know each other eventually anyway, but still, give credit where...). Having talked her roommates into meeting Bill, who at the time was drumming for the WUOGers, an unserious group of local college radio DJs, Michael Stipe was impressed by the drummer's "eyebrows, or eyebrow." Neither Stipe nor Buck initially thought

Above: Michael Stipe's interest in folk art was made manifest from the beginning of the band's career. This photo is from an early video made by local artist Jim Herbert; it's set in a field of folk art "sculptures."

Right: It's easy to sense a certain ambiguity on the part of the R.E.M. boys toward their hard-won fame and fortune.

much of Mike Mills, who didn't go out of his way to impress, but the rhythm section was a package deal. At the time, Michael and Peter had discussed getting together as well with Paul Butchart and Kit Swartz, of the future Side Effects. But that never came together.

"We were friends, we all were playing instruments, and we were talking about starting a band," recalls Peter Buck. "I think we actually, at one point, had made the time to get together with Paul and Kit and practice and they didn't show up. It wasn't like this huge urge to be stars, you know? It just seemed like everyone else was doing it. It seemed like a lot of fun. And music was what we liked."

Even the fateful first session with Berry and Mills took a few abortive arrangements to actually come off, though once it did the result proved satisfactory to all concerned. Mike and Bill had written some songs that they then showed Michael and Peter. Mike liked the way Peter played them on guitar despite that, technically, Mills was a much more proficient player. But Peter's very ineptitude, coupled with his natural bent toward '60s minimalist guitar, lent his playing a unique flavor that appealed to Mills, who had long ago become bored of the typical masturbatory guitar playing he and Bill encountered in their cover band days. The rapidly coalescing combo quickly whipped up a few more very basic originals (very

unlike those on the band's first EP, *Chronic Town*) and a bevy of covers, and they were on their way.

Not too long before their first-ever show, after having played together with Bill and Mike for about three weeks, Michael and Peter took time out for a spring break (the two were both still in school at the time), their first-ever trip to New York with Paul Butchart of the soon-to-be Side Effects and mutual friend and record collector Kurt Wood. The quartet drove to the Big Apple in the old green van, fairly unprepared for the culture shock necessarily attendant on such a trip. All they knew was that Pylon was playing and they wanted to go to New York and see the band. As it turns out, the week-long adventure (described by all parties as a wild time) provided Buck with the chance to meet one of his long-time idols, legendary rock critic Lester Bangs.

Above: As with any band, successful or not, the story of R.E.M. contains a hell of a lot of "what ifs." And maybe even a dollop of luck.

Right: A moody, word-struck young geek, Michael Stipe by his own account was a painfully shy individual whose best friends were his sisters.

Overleaf: Neither Michael Stipe nor Peter Buck initially thought much of Mike Mills, who met them dead reeling drunk. But the rhythm section was a package deal.

FRONT LINES

Hot Night In Athens, Ga.

ATHENS, GA – Scenemakers in this danceable Dixie town known for its inordinate number of rock and roll bands last month saw an end to an Athens tradition when **Tyrone's O.C.** ("Old Chameleon," a previous name for the club) went up in flames in the early morning hours of January 8. News of the blaze spread through town almost as quickly as the flames, and that morning many local bands were already asking, "Where are we gonna play now?!"

A list of losses not only includes the much-used sound system and some band equipment left in Tyrone's after the last performance, but also some of the funkiest girl's room graffiti in the South.

Tyrone's O.C. was a club that changed with the times in Athens. Built in an abandoned warehouse near the old railroad, the club first featured a small corner stage, just a step up from the audience, on which mostly folk and blues combos performed. As more innovative local rock and roll began to emerge, Tyrone's became one of the first clubs willing to book the bands creating this new sound.

Over the next two years, walls were torn down and the small stage elevated and elongated into a full-sized one. With the larger stage came a larger dance floor, a second bar, and record crowds. It's unlikely the club will be immediately resurrected, as its owners had no insurance on the rickety property. Benefit performances have been organized by various bands and other clubs to help offset the financial loss.

Another kind of loss will be felt by everyone who frequented the place for a straight shot of alcohol and rock (though I'm sure regular patrons won't mourn the destruction of their bar tabs). But the greatest impact will be on the bands that played Tyrone's, and on new combos seeking exposure and experience there. As Mike Mills of REM told *NY Rocker*, "The guys at Tyrone's, they provided a place for somebody to get up and do something different." For now, those Athens groups seeking to "do something different" will have to do it at the infamous 40-Watt Club, which has been experiencing a booming post-fire business.

by Sandra-Lee Phipps

ASHES TO ASHES, FUNK TO FUNKY: Tyrone's in ruins, the morning after the blaze.

"I met him at a party at a friend of Pylon's house who we knew, too," recalls Peter. "The people from Pylon said, 'Oh we can't make it, we're sound-checking. Why don't you go?' We said, 'Okay, sure.' We didn't realize that it was only like an eight-person party. It was Lester Bangs, Joe 'King' Carasco and his band, this girl Karen, whose house it was, and us. And everyone was like, 'God, you're the people from Georgia we've been hearing about.' We'd been living in this van and none of us had bathed. We were wearing makeup and stuff. None of us had eaten in days. We just had no idea how much things cost in New York. We were assuming we could eat a meal for a dollar-fifty like we could in Georgia, so we ran out of money on about the second day. After that, we just kind of depended on the kindness of strangers. Lester Bangs was at that party and he was as drunk as he could possibly be. It was kind of like a Zen thing. He'd stand in this hallway and when you'd walk by he would say some personal insult, just to you: 'You rotten piece of shit.' I think he called me a rotten cocksucker—but it wasn't personal.

"We met Joe 'King' there, too, and he took us out. We hadn't eaten in days and he took me and Michael out for pizza. He said, 'Oh yeah, are you guys hungry?' We thought it was the biggest thing in the world, to give us three dollars for slices of pizza."

Back in Athens, desultorily preparing for its debut (the band had to be talked into playing by Bill's then-girlfriend Kathleen), R.E.M. ordered pizza and beer and played and played.

April 5, 1980: In a ramshackle desanctified church on Oconee Street, some boho college types are throwing a party. Three bands are on the unofficial "bill," two of which are making their debuts: The Side Effects, made up of three popular art students, Paul Butchart, Kit Swartz, and Jimmy Ellison (husband of Pylon's Vanessa), and an as yet unnamed (tonight they go by the temporary moniker Twisted Kites) combo that had been rehearsing for about three weeks in the church. This last band consisted of two ecclesiastical residents, Peter Buck and Michael Stipe, and a rhythm section of recently transplanted Maconians, Bill Berry and Mike Mills.

By all accounts, this unabashedly non-sober party was a grand success; few remember the soon-defunct opening band, Turtle Bay, but the Side Effects were immediately popular and henceforth highly influential in Athens's "bomp and stomp" scene, of which R.E.M. was also marginally a part. Their sharp, concise, extremely danceworthy, and highly unserious approach to art-school pop à la Pylon went over gangbusters and would soon make them local heroes.

Above: One harbinger of the end of the first stage of the Athens music scene was the night in 1982 when Tyrones burned down.

Right: R.E.M.'s earliest sets consisted of at least half covers, including the Monkees' "Stepping Stone" and the Velvet Underground's "There She Goes Again."

The final band to perform was less immediately popular, although many at the party were doubtless too soused to pass judgment at that point. Its set consisted of at least half cover songs, including the Monkees' "Stepping Stone" and the Velvet Underground's "There She Goes Again." Playing cover songs was naturally frowned upon by the way-hip Athens art crowd, who prized originality above, well, quality. But this new band managed to captivate enough members of the audience that it was suggested they find themselves an official name and play more gigs. Dennis Greenia, who helped run Rick the Printer's 11:11 Klub, a kind of bohemian coffee bar (whose hippie motto was "Do you know where your coffee is?") offered the band a nonpaying show in two weeks, which the band used as a warmup for their third and final nonpaying gig, opening for the Brains, a new wave combo from Atlanta, at Tyrone's. (Tyrone's booker, Mike Hobbs, was also at the party and was also impressed.)

The newly named R.E.M. (they picked the name from the dictionary, mainly for its nonspecific gist) blew away the hapless Brains, who— let's be fair—pretty much sucked anyway. The band was given a headlining spot one week later and pulled in an astonishing 350 people—more than three times the number art-school and critic darlings Pylon usually drew. That date, May 12, just over one month since the band's debut at the

church party, marked the end of the carefree stage of the Athens music scene. Heretofore the scene had been a closed one, where everyone who went to the shows pretty much knew each other. R.E.M. broadened the audience by drawing from the frat boys and sorority girls, kids who tended to drink more and dance less. The art kids stopped coming to R.E.M. shows because they were too crowded and no one was dancing. It just wasn't fun anymore.

"We came out of a scene," says a reminiscing Peter Buck, "that everyone firmly believed in and your goal was not to be a rock star. You didn't dress up. You didn't have a stage show. You didn't have witty stage patter. You just kind of played. The people who came to see you, by and large, at least in the early days, were your friends. There were only about eighty of us in town. We were the first band to go beyond that to the college kids.

So it was all of us. Everyone dressed in these thrift store rags. Make-your-own-costume-type people. And so you'd go and dance. . . . You know, we were real popular here, but the audience might

Above: A rare glimpse of Michael Stipe at home.

Right: Stipe's obstinate productivity is one of the main motors that drives R.E.M. His creativity can't be contained within the confines of the band.

not look at the stage the entire set. It was really kind of fun, loose. And we'd drag people out of the audience onstage to come and dance with us.

"Our friends stopped coming to see us. They'd go, 'Goddamn, we can't dance anymore. It's all these college kids that worship you.' And I'm not complaining at all, but where we came from, we were just doing this thing and everyone else was doing this thing. And it was supposed to be enjoyable. We were considered a pop band in those days. We were. Everyone else was getting harder, so we were poppy. It was, like, That's okay. The next band that opened for us might be a trombone and a snare drum. People danced, to that. We had fire eaters open for us. Jugglers. We had an Irish folk band. It was kind of like, Oh, that's cool. It's all from the same place. Then it got kind of, Oh, look at the band. They're famous. People start asking for your autograph and stuff."

The summer of 1980 was, according to those who lived through it, a nonstop party. It was an exciting time for the Athens music scene; bands had sprouted up in the wake of the B-52's seemingly all over the place, and all of them were cool, and everyone was friends, and the future was impossibly luminous (because it didn't exist, or was fuzzed by the daze of alcohol and drugs). The scene in those days centered around a number of houses on Barber Street where a good portion of the scene's brain trust resided and threw parties,

not necessarily in that order. Barber Street became known as the Street of the Stars after a couple of drunken girls one night, in a patch of conveniently wet sidewalk cement along that stretch of houses, scrawled the names of the street's resident notables: Pylon, R.E.M., the Side Effects, Love Tractor. The names are still there today. Go look.

"Basically, the whole scene was where the guys might wear dresses," comments Peter Buck. "At one point, I think all of us in Athens bands have worn dresses. So we'd go to parties and what everyone always played was James Brown and the Ventures. I don't know why. The B's loved him, Side Effects' Paul Butchart had great James Brown and Ventures collections. So you'd go to these parties and everyone would get drunk and dance on tables and take their clothes off and they'd be playing all James Brown and the Ventures. I don't know why we didn't all end up sounding like James Brown—although, you can definitely hear it in Pylon."

Above: Peter Buck: "We came out of a scene that everyone firmly believed in, and your goal was not to be a rock star."

Right: "You just kind of played. The people who came to see you in the early days, by and large, were your friends."

Overleaf: "We were considered a pop band in those days. We were. Everyone else was getting harder, so we were poppy."

Sat. 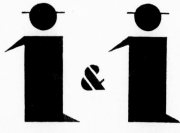 Feb 12

Athens' Progressive Music Club
244 Oconee Street • 548-8388

R.E.M.

For People 19 or Younger
No Alcohol Allowed
Doors Open 7 pm   Show 8.30 pm

Michael Stipe was particularly busy this summer, playing not only with the factory-fresh R.E.M., but with his embarrassing cover band Gangster, which he quit soon after and made friends swear never to disclose his involvement in (it didn't, apparently, work) a solo project called 1066 Gaggle o' Sound that consisted of Michael reading words over a beat-up, messed-with Farfisa organ accompaniment, Tanzplagen, with local guitarist Lee Self, and Boat Of, with local art-noise enthusiast Tom Smith, who thought Michael was cool until he heard R.E.M. and who later formed a band called Peach of Immortality in Washington, D.C., that released an album called R.E.M. = Air Supply (and printed up T-shirts reading A COLLECTIVE FIST UP M. STIPE'S ASS). But his involvement in these side projects soon became limited at best, as R.E.M. consumed more and more of his time. The band did its best to play as many shows both in town and out of town as possible; on one of its increasingly frequent road trips it met its manager-to-be, Jefferson Holt. Holt was so impressed by the band's show at the Station in Carrboro, North Carolina, that he eventually moved to Athens, taking responsibility for booking the band and handling the money off the hands of Bill Berry, who until then had handled most of the business end with his girlfriend Kathleen O'Brien. The band also received astute legal advice from Bert

Downs, who advised R.E.M. to incorporate early on and helped them negotiate their first record deal with Johnny Hibbert for the Hib-Tone "Radio Free Europe" single. Later he would come to comanage the band with Jefferson.

Bertis Downs IV first saw R.E.M. at the post-church Koffee Klub gig where the police came and shut down the band's set; he became an immediate and lasting fan, telling the neophyte and hardly (at that point) career-minded band that it was going to be "bigger than the Beatles." Needless to say, no one believed him then, least of all the band. And anyway, the very thought was repulsive—who wanted to be that big?

As with any band, successful or not, the story of R.E.M. contains a hell of a lot of what ifs. What if Peter Buck had never taken the job at the Athens's Wuxtry, where he met and befriended the notoriously shy Michael Stipe? What if Michael and Peter had gotten together with Paul Butchart and Kit Swartz of the Side Effects, as the four had planned, instead of Mike Mills and Bill Berry? What if Bill Berry hadn't previously worked for

Above: The summer of 1980 was reported by those who lived through it to be a non-stop party.

Right: Peter Buck: "I think we were the first band that Ian Copeland's booking agency, F.B.I., had ever signed that didn't have a record deal."

Ian Copeland of the F.B.I. booking agency, facilitating both their ability to tour and, eventually, their record deal with Ian's brother Miles' record company, I.R.S.? What if Bill had decided to stay in Love Tractor rather than R.E.M.?

And as with any band, successful or not, these intangibles ultimately have very little to do with their fate, for good or for ill. R.E.M.'s success was predicated on its appetite for hard work; the band began from an undeniably qualified foundation, but without the indefatigable willingness to put in the miles, touring up and down and all around at a time when that was unheard of, especially for a band without a record deal, it never would have "made it." Willingness—hell, they were eager to tour. If ever a band lived for the road it was R.E.M. in those early days.

"Once you start playing out of town," comments Peter Buck, "it seems a whole lot better than working. I could go back and be a janitor or work at the newspaper or at the record store or we could go on tour. Who in their right mind wouldn't want to go on tour? And as far as that goes, if we stayed home, we'd be writing songs over time and be practicing. And we might as well do this, not in a more professional way, but just do it more often, being forced to be together all the time traveling.

"I mean, we all had shit jobs. We were gone every weekend, so we couldn't work weekends. All of us, we started being gone on Thursdays. All of us, if we didn't lose our jobs, we were getting to the point where we weren't making any money anyway. Come back and work two days. At

a certain point it just seems silly."

Whatever the motivations, the endless roadwork began fairly soon to pay dividends.

"All of a sudden, people from record companies were talking to us," recalls Peter, " 'cause we were drawing a thousand people a night all through the South and no one had ever heard of us. Mark Williams who was a DJ down at 688 was an intern at I.R.S. who called Jay Boberg. As well as one of Bill's friends, Ian Copeland. All these people had found out about us through word of mouth. 'These guys are drawing well. They have good songs.'

"I think we were the first band that Ian's booking agent, F.B.I., had ever signed that didn't have a record deal. We used to send tapes to Ian, 'cause Bill had worked for him in the '70s. It was when Ian brought over the Damned and Squeeze, and his southern rock pals were like, 'You're full of shit. This punk stuff ain't going nowhere.' And Ian was really excited about it. So we'd send tapes.

"And Ian didn't do us any favors. He'd listen to the tapes. He said, 'They're pretty good. They're not produced very well.' Then he'd like throw us a gig. He'd get us a date for a hundred bucks opening for Bow Wow Wow somewhere. It was one of those things where he liked Bill and he thought the band was interesting. He'd seen us play and he

Above: So R.E.M. toured and toured, and at one point decided to put out that one great single: "Radio Free Europe" b/w "Sitting Still" on friend and big fan Johnny Hibbert's nascent Hib-Tone label.

was willing to give us a little hand. But he actually, literally signed us to a contract before we had a record deal."

R.E.M.'s newfound success, however limited, took a little bit of adjusting to on the part of a band who had very specifically never had any notion of doing anything other than paying its rent by playing music. R.E.M. was one of the few Athens bands, in fact, that refused to heed the siren call to go play in New York City—the path to instant success for the B-52's and Pylon—until relatively late in the game, preferring to play the pizza parlors and discos of its gradually broadening southeastern circuit.

"I think maybe some of the Athens bands realized, a little better than we did, how you can go about getting a deal," concurs Buck. "You know, you could go to New York, put out records, you just need to have contacts and all that sort of stuff. We were younger than the rest of the people in the scene and not quite from the same art school–type things. We were not like outsiders, but all the contacts everybody else took for granted, we didn't really have.

"Plus, our goals were a little different, I guess. One great single—that's what we wanted. No one expects a hit. You've got to remember that the idea that you could do that for more than like a year was just unheard of. I guess everyone had seen the Beatles and Stones and stuff, but down here it was—ideally, we were thinking, well, we could play once a month in town, make a couple hundred bucks. And maybe every couple of years or so, we'd put out an EP or a single. For a lot of the bands that I've followed from the punk era since, it wasn't a career. It was something they did. And they didn't have videos and makeup artists and stuff. So we figured, if we got really lucky and we're good at this, then we can play. And maybe in the next five or six years, we could put out an album and a couple of singles and an EP."

So R.E.M. toured and toured, and at one point they decided to put out that one great single, "Radio Free Europe" b/w "Sitting Still," on friend and big fan Johnny Hibbert's nascent Hib-Tone label. The record, released in July 1981 after the first turbulent year of R.E.M.-hood, brought in-

creased critical attention, especially from the hip New York rags, but little in the way of obvious audience enhancement. That would continue to come only by virtue of constant, never-ending, indefatigable touring. Four band members and one manager in an old green Dodge van ("We had this green van we'd bought from these older guys, like fifty years old," remembers Buck. "They were fishermen. It was kind of like a fifty-year-old guy's idea of what a real bitchin' van would be, like shag carpet on the ceilings, an eight-track player."), crisscrossing a growing portion of jerkwater America; and every time they went back there were a few more fans.

The culmination of all the ceaseless work occurred on March 12, 1980, when Jay Boberg, the young president of I.R.S., happened to be in New Orleans the same night as an R.E.M. gig and decided to see for himself if the band was for real.

"Yeah, in New Orleans, on Bourbon Street, I think," recalls Peter Buck. "A place called Beat Exchange. The lady that ran it was nice. I actually know some of her friends now. Her name was Barbara something-or-other. I walked into the bathroom and there was this syringe. Someone had darted into the wall. I just went, 'Uhhh . . . eww.' There were only like six people there. And there was a Rasta sound guy who would go out when the time was right and have 'the herb, mon.' So we'd be playing away and there'd be no sound guy. He'd leave this incense burning to show that his spirit was there. So it was basically Barbara, him, and Jay.

"We were sitting there after we'd done the set and this guy comes back and goes, 'Hi. I'm Jay Boberg.' And Michael went, 'Oh man, we were hoping you wouldn't come.' Because all our equipment broke down, like, four times. The sound guy would leave and there'd be feedback for five minutes. No one was there. There was a fist fight during the set. People were going and shooting up in the bathrooms. But he listened for what he listened for."

And what he heard, he liked. Two months later, R.E.M. signed to I.R.S. (May 31, 1982) and agreed to release the already-recorded EP *Chronic Town*. American music would never be the same.

R.E.M.

C H A P T E R   2

T H E   B I R T H   O F
C O L L E G E   R O C K
1 9 8 2 – 1 9 8 3

THE BIRTH OF COLLEGE ROCK

Contrary to popular belief—if you consider *Rolling Stone* magazine a fair measure of popular belief—R.E.M. is not "America's Best Rock & Roll Band." Fact is, R.E.M. is hardly a rock band at all. It started out as a folk-pop cover band and converted after a while to a brilliant pop group, brilliant above all in its consistency. R.E.M. has quite simply never put out a bad album, which is something very few bands of similar longevity and stature can claim. Nevertheless consistency does not greatness make, and by the obverse token, the band has yet to pull off a truly great album—what Peter Buck would consider one of the "twenty best, all-time, rock'n'roll records," a goal publicly acknowledged.

But R.E.M. is not really the best band, only because the notion of a best band is absurd; on any given night, any of a hundred groups can lay claim to that title and not very many of these sound like R.E.M. The group's importance to the development of American rock music in the 1980s cannot be underestimated, but its role was largely as catalyst, and was no more crucial, than that of, say, the Los Angeles hardcore band Black Flag, although R.E.M. was influential on a much more accessible level. The band was "the acceptable edge of the unacceptable stuff," Buck once told *Rolling Stone*, which alone was a lot, but really that

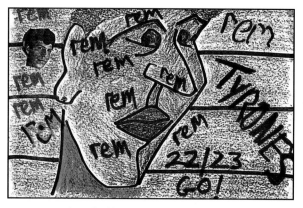

statement low-balls R.E.M.'s impact. For better or worse, R.E.M. is responsible for an entire genre of music—"college rock"—that did not exist, at least in any organized sense, before the band did. R.E.M. ushered it in, and, by growing beyond its narrow strictures, by becoming more successful than the most ambitious college rock band had dared fancy, R.E.M. ushered it out. "College rock" is today an outdated, meaningless marketing term (whereas it once was a trendy, meaningless marketing term). Its development is inextricably intertwined with that of R.E.M., and its story is,

in fair measure, the band's story, too.

In 1979, most college radio stations played what you could safely call "hippie music" without getting, like, shot. This format had the advantage of great eclecticism—in any given hour, you could hear Stravinsky followed by Robert Johnson followed by Captain Beefheart followed by Miles Davis; the music was always good, at least in a Special K kind of "good for you" sense, but you couldn't (usually) dance to it and it wasn't exactly an accurate reflection of what young college kids were listening to. A few adventurous programmers had begun playing punk and new wave when they started happening in 1976 or so, but in general, rock of any sort was frowned on by the highbrow hippies.

Remember, too, that college radio stations were at that time very much fringe outfits that subsisted on benevolent support from the administration and the community. The massive college rock promo network gradually established over the next decade did not exist, and the station's record library, built up over time by purchases and donations, was often supplemented by the individual DJ's personal collection. Stations did not have playlists as did commercial concerns, dictating what records could or could not be played. Without advertising to rely on, and consequently ratings to worry about, there wasn't a need for playlists. Which, after all, was the whole point of college radio.

Above: R.E.M. made it a point to visit every Podunk college radio station in every Podunk town they played.

Right: Shortly after **Murmur**'s *debut, Michael Stipe began to be plagued with the "mystic young poet" tag that would follow him for the rest of his career.*

But beginning in the early '80s, all that changed. More and more, DJs began playing the new middle-class, white-boy art-school music ("college rock" was really a deliberately noncommercial extrapolation from the old middle-class, white-boy, art-school music, i.e., Roxy Music, T. Rex, Nick Drake, and, further back, the Kinks) of which R.E.M. was the most obvious and successful example. And success, as we all know, breeds record company sleaze. As soon as the major labels hepped to the fact that a) there was money to be made from some of the up-and-coming college rock bands, especially the ones that sound like

R.E.M., and that b) an easy way to see which ones were up-and-coming was to keep track of what was being played on college radio, the jig was basically up. Not until later did college radio turn

Above: Official fan club postcard including manager Jefferson Holt (far left) and lawyer Bertis Downs (far right). R.E.M. made every effort to include Holt and Downs as fifth and sixth members of the band, rather than as employees.

Right: An R.E.M. Christmas card, featuring the band members as well as Holt, Downs, office staff Liz Holt and Sandra Lee-Phipps, and tour manager Curtis Goodman.

into an effective marketing tool for whatever completely manufactured "alternative" band the company had managed to spew out that week, but the groundwork for radio's homogenization was laid in those early days, much as it had been for FM radio in the late '60s.

And again, however unwittingly, this is partly R.E.M.'s fault. Put it down to the band's dauntless work ethic and the astuteness of the band's management—the band from very early on understood that its natural constituency lay with adherents of college radio and made it a point to visit every Podunk station in every Podunk town it played. In those days, the most effective way of promoting an R.E.M. gig would be to do an interview on the college station—most of the kids who would like-

ly be interested would probably be tuned in. Doubtless if the group knew that by pioneering the use of college radio as a promotional tool it had hastened its demise, it would have been aghast.

Especially since R.E.M.'s debt to the very net-

Above: That R.E.M. has yet to succumb to mediocrity is a tribute both to the band's innate talent and to whatever large, scary monster drives it to do what it does in the first place.

Right: Each member of the band has a snugly fitting role. Mike Mills is the most accomplished musician and handles a lot of the arranging. Michael Stipe is responsible for words and images and brags of his unfamiliarity with standard musical concepts.

work it helped to nurture was immense. It's not too much to say that without college radio, R.E.M. would never have enjoyed the success it did through the first half of the '80s, when commercial radio wouldn't have touched the band with a ten-thousand-foot transmitter.

Even before R.E.M. had signed with I.R.S., the band had decided to record an EP of some of the new material it had worked up in the last year or so. The experience of recording the "Radio Free Europe" single at Mitch Easter's Drive-In Studio in Winston-Salem, North Carolina (after an abortive session at a studio in Atlanta) had proved satisfactory enough that the band was determined to return. R.E.M. had agreed that a friend and avid fan, David Healey, would put up the money for the three-day, five-song recording session, at which the band bashed through "1,000,000," "Gardening at Night," "Carnival of Sorts (Boxcars)," "Stumble," and "Ages of You" (the last of which was dropped for a later-recorded "Wolves, Lower" on the I.R.S.-released EP). Healey wanted to start a label called Dasht Hopes, and intended to use the R.E.M. EP as his first release. So the band set off in October 1981 for North Carolina.

Or, at least, it tried to. The recording of *Chronic Town* actually almost didn't happen, for purely prosaic reasons. The old green Dodge van broke down yet again on the eve of the recording date at Mitch Easter's Drive-In Studio, leaving the band with time booked but no method of transportation. Hardly any of their friends in Athens could afford cars. Anyone, that is, except the band's old friend Kurt Wood, a tall, Afro-coiffed scenester whose splinter-thin pogoing frame could be seen down front at almost every cool rock show in town.

"We'd known Kurt for a million years," says Peter, remembering. "He used to come into the record store I worked at, and we were good friends. So we had Kurt in his little Volvo....He said, 'Well, I was gonna go record shopping anyway.' So, I think we paid for his gas and gave him thirty dollars or something. He drove us up, and he'd go out while we were recording. He'd go drive around to thrift shops and find these great, weird records. We only went there for three days. It seems like it was a month, but I think it was Friday and Saturday and half of Sunday."

Chronic Town is the first burp of a still-teething band; it sounds, still, like the hastily scrabbled work of four kids who can't believe they got to make a record and want to get it down quick before they get caught. Nevertheless, the EP contains, in seed form, every musical flower R.E.M.

would eventually produce. *Chronic Town* also serves as the opening move of the college rock game—laying down the rules later slavishly copied by any number of less-talented devotees, who thought that, yeah, all we need is a fistful of guitar jangle and some moany incomprehensible vocals and the babes and bucks will be ours. For one thing, the vocals are neither moany nor incomprehensible (see below), and for another thing if guitar jangle were the key, the Feelies and the dBs would have been big stars (not to mention Big Star). While it's maybe not exactly true that R.E.M. invented college rock (any more than the Beatles invented psychedelia), they certainly codified (and perhaps accessorized) it.

A couple of points concerning the EP: 1) Vocals. The vocals are not incomprehensible, nor are they buried in the mix. They are sometimes slurred to the point of indistinction, but repeated listenings yield all but a few recalcitrant syllables. The level

Above: This fan club postcard depicts the album cover of 1983's Murmur *without the lettering. Kudzu. Ugly.*

Right: Peter Buck is R.E.M.'s rock 'n' roll fanatic. He has one of the largest record collections in the free world. Bill Berry at one time handled the lion's share of the band's business dealings, before Jefferson Holt came on board.

arpeggiating and the enigmatic (read: nonsensical) line "Suspicion yourself, suspicion yourself, don't get caught." From there the song falls forward into a wordless chorus underpinned by backing vocals intoning "house in order." (Another soon-to-be trademark would be the wordless-croon chorus.) The break is spiced with some backward guitar noodling before lurching back into the verse; the whole thing has a tacked-together, haphazard feel that adds greatly to its effect. Just as the lyrics are a patchwork quilt of sense and nonsense stitched together primarily out of regard for their assonance or consonance, so the musical arrangement takes the basic building blocks of "rock" music and rearranges them, with Mike Mills's melodic (and weirdly harmonic—ignoring almost completely the chord structure dictated by the guitar, and instead, following the vocal line) bass taking the place sometimes of the vocal melody and sometimes of the guitar melody, and Peter Buck chopping up the known vocabulary of rock'n'roll guitar and resplicing it together seemingly at random. The wonder of it is, it works.

"Gardening at Night" follows next with a similar deconstruction, only this time in a far folkier vein, meshing acoustic and electric guitars together to great effect, as R.E.M. would often do in the future. The song takes familiar chords and makes them sound fresh by virtue of the arrangement's unaffected simplicity—where another band might take the same progression and gussy it up with a complicated arrangement designed to hide its inherent ordinariness, R.E.M. revels in the standard progression, pulling from it every ounce of its resident resonance. Michael Stipe croons in a much-higher-than-usual key, giving "Gardening" an unusual delicacy. Stipe once allowed that some people think the song's enigmatic lyrics are "about my father, some people think they're about drugs, and some people think they're about gardening at night. They're about all of them."

The mysterious swirling organ that announces "Carnival of Sorts (Box Cars)" also announces one of the finest songs the band has ever put down on tape. The chorus's repeated "Boxcars are turning out of town," while no less mysterious than the bulk of Stipe's early writing, is used here to unusually evocative effect—the phrase's sense of melancholic change underscores the plangent feel

of the vocals in the mix might be a tad lower than standard AOR fare, but only a tad, and many bands before and since have buried their vocals a lot more successfully. That said, the lyrics still don't make a heck of a lot of linear "sense." But I can't understand why this kind of thing would be misunderstood as "poetry" when all it really is is just a tighter version of a fine old prog-rock tradition—dare I say, cliché? (Think Yes, "I Am the Walrus," Rush, et cetera)—reapplied to postpunk song structure. No big deal, you'd think. You'd be wrong. 2) Guitar. Peter Buck might have had a limited stylistic palette, guitar-wise, but all contemporary reports to the contrary, he certainly could play. When you consider his apprenticeship included a couple hundred live shows stretched over the preceding two years, there's very little chance the man would not have picked up some sort of rudimentary competence. Especially on the five songs included here. That he chose to employ his competence in such a minimalistic manner bespeaks an exercise of taste, not a limitation of ability (it's a lesson his later imitators would often fail to learn).

"Wolves, Lower" starts the record off with a soon-to-be trademark burst of Rickenbacker

---

Above: Another early R.E.M. flyer. The band had played literally hundreds of shows by the time Murmur *was recorded.*

Right: Michael Stipe: "There's only a certain degree to which someone who doesn't actually know you can understand you."

of the arrangement. "Carnival" also contains the "chronic town" phrase from which the EP derived its title. There's a neat twelve-string guitar figure in the chorus, as well, which is probably where a lot of critics decided that R.E.M. showed a heavy Byrds influence, despite that the band was hardly well-acquainted with its supposed influence's work. The worst thing about the song, and in fact, about the EP in general, is Stipe's clenched-throat singing, which at times sounds forced. In fact, in 1990, when I asked Michael what his least favorite thing about the early records was, he replied unhesitatingly, "The singing." Nevertheless, once he learned to moderate his voice, the inherent reediness of his singing became its most appealing quality.

The intro to "1,000,000" is the most rock-sounding thing on the EP (it sounds to me like a wimpier version of Led Zep's "Communication Breakdown"). The song then devolves into a folky bridge and chorus, containing one of Stipe's more straightforward lyrics: "I could live a million years."

"Stumble," the EP's last number, is also one of the EP's most interesting, stylistically. After a snaky drum-and-harmonics intro, complete with Bill Berry's ace roto-tom fills, Peter Buck launches into a guitar figure in the style of Keith Levene (from early Public Image Ltd.) on the chorus. Very new wave. You can also hear Michael Stipe laughing just before the song starts, uttering the single word "teeth" and snapping his jaws a couple of times into the microphone.

As limited and inchoate as *Chronic Town* might sound to ears numbed by '90s "production values" (an execrable farce that has been perpetrated on you, the hapless consumer, from above—but that's another story), R.E.M. has never since produced anything as fresh or innovative. Even *Murmur's* neofolk meshings fail to match the EP's energy, drive, and creative spark. Which is not to say that it's been all downhill since, just that things change. And it's an old story, nevertheless true, that you never really match the first blind thrashings of your youth. Once you figure out what you're doing you become "professional" and therefore doomed to eventual mediocrity. That R.E.M. has yet to succumb (despite its self-mocking video compilation from a few years later) is tribute both to the band's innate talent and to whatever large, scary monster drives it to do what it does in the first place.

Whatever monster that might turn out to be, it's certainly not money. The band has been accused at every instance in its career of selling

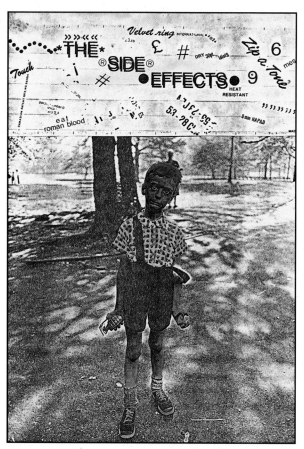

out, from the moment it signed with I.R.S. to its appearance at 1991's Grammy Awards. But one thing R.E.M. has never done is sell out—at least, in any commonly understood sense of the term. It's natural, if you're a performer of any sort, to want to see your work distributed on as wide a scale as possible; the only time that becomes "selling out" is when the performer agrees to make artistic compromises in order to achieve this wider distribution. R.E.M. has never made compromises, musically. Whether you like the band's music or not, it has always conceived and executed it exactly as it wanted, with an almost remarkable lack of direction from the record company.

Peter, it's often been said that after your initial success, all of a sudden, there was this big explosion of R.E.M. clones. That college radio was transformed by your success. How do you respond to those claims?

Above: Poster from the very first R.E.M. show (under the name Twisted Kites - not listed here, though versions of this flyer reportedly did exist listing that name) at the church on Oconee Street on April 5, 1980.

Facing: R.E.M.'s early live show was a particularly kinetic experience. Here, Stipe's pants appear to move even while the singer is standing still!

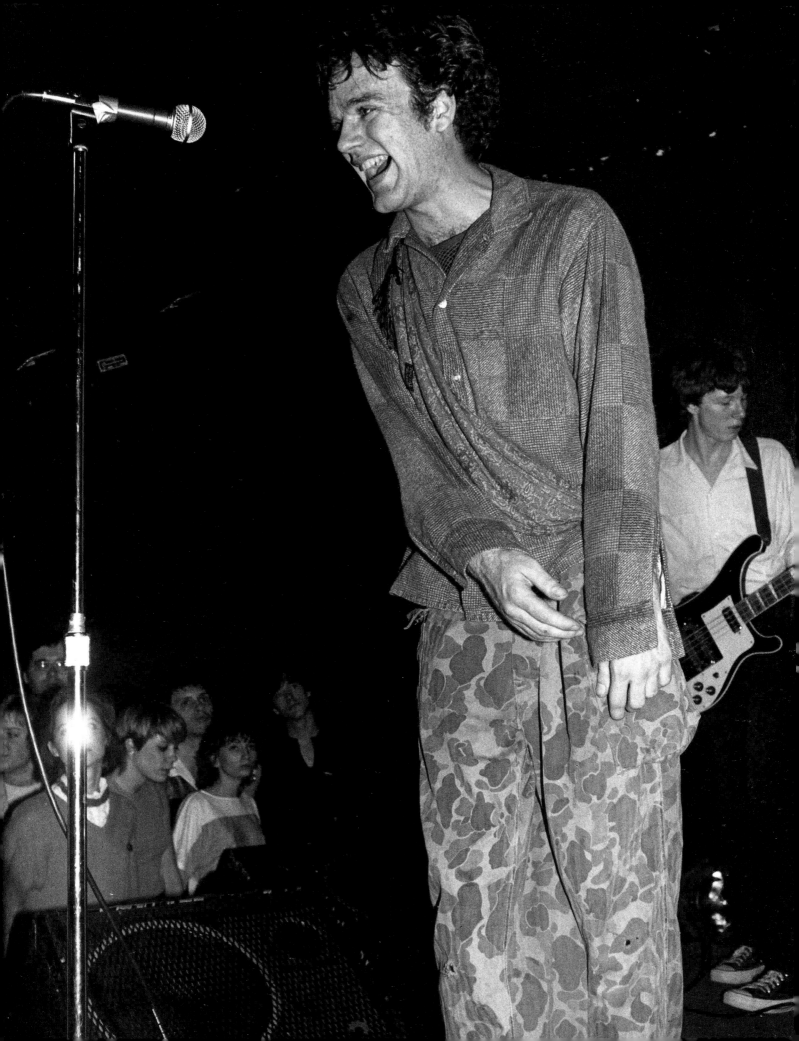

Buck: You know, I kind of miss those days. You'd listen, you'd hear like Olantunji followed by a jazz record. Now it seems all college radio plays are white kids under thirty. And I think that's doing a big disservice to the listenership.

But about R.E.M. clones: Thing is, you've got to remember that there's a bunch of Sonic Youth clone bands now. Even though they've never sold records, at least, in the sense that someone like U2 sells records. Rather than someone imitating the sound of a band, what people tended to imitate, to be influenced by, was the idea. And maybe the less creative or able people will imitate the sound, too. But I talk to lots of kids, like Ed [Crawford] from Firehose [which features ex-Minutemen George Hurley and Mike Watt]. We were his biggest influence until he saw the Minutemen. And he saw the Minutemen open for us. Isn't that a great little story? And his stuff doesn't really sound like us or anything. The intelligent people take it and push it. What they take is the idea: Well, here's this new way of doing this thing. And after us, it was the Replacements and Sonic Youth. I'll bet you this year it will be Nirvana.

In the sense you mean, Nirvana was a Sonic Youth clone band, anyway.

Right. They don't take the sound, they take the attitude, the idea.

Buck's assertions to the contrary, the college

radio airwaves from very early on—say, just after the release of *Murmur*—began to be deluged with ringing Rickenbackers and keening, tortured pseudopoetic vocals. Bands with "clever" names, such as Other Bright Colors and Miracle Legion, took more than just the iconoclastic spirit from R.E.M., they took part of the musical idiom as well. The only problem was, they didn't get it right; R.E.M.'s success might in the harshest light be looked at as the result of a consistently applied formula, but the elements of that formula are essential to the whole. Most of the bands who followed in R.E.M.'s footsteps failed because they tried to improve on an unimprovable concept—by making the song structure more complex, or the guitar-playing less one-dimensional, or the singing more soulful or more melodic—thus mucking up the very thing that was appealing about the R.E.M. sound: its simplicity.

Others failed, conversely, because their songs weren't melodic or appealing enough, as if they thought that chiming guitars and random moans were enough in themselves to make you famous. Although "becoming famous" was purportedly the last thing on these bands' agendas, an awful lot of griping ensued when R.E.M.'s star kept rising,

Above: Shortly after Murmur's *release, the college radio airwaves begun to be deluged with ringing Rickenbackers and keening, tortured pseudopoetic vocals.*

and theirs kept, um, not.

Others didn't fail, but mutated past the slavish-devotion phase into something more original, or at least more appealing. Long-time R.E.M. faves Drivin'-n-Cryin', for instance (whose lead singer and guitarist Kevin Kinney is a frequent Peter Buck collaborator), chose a harder, rootsier path than the one frequented by their pals, and have carved out a swell mid-level career for themselves (with the potential for even greater things).

In any case, the proliferation of clones, while not as thoroughly noxious as nuclear proliferation, made listening to college radio a hit-or-miss prospect for much of the early- to mid-'80s. At the time, a quick perusal of the biweekly review section in *College Music Journal (CMJ)* would provide an amusing lesson in creative writing as the staff's writers sought new ways to say "R.E.M.-influenced" or "sounds like R.E.M." (Among other sobriquets, they'd resort to "that band from Georgia" and "that southern group that sounds like the Byrds.")

Michael Stipe remembers a different college radio than the one that developed in the wake of his band's success: "We used to storm the college radio station here in Athens, and we would play, like, the Banana Splits song and then a Throbbing Gristle song. The show would have a group theme, and we would play music for hours and hours and come on the air every once in a while and, like, bark.

"I recall one day in particular when the rock'n'roll show was supposed to end and the jazz show start, and the jazz guy called up and said, 'I've got a flat tire and I'm gonna be about fifteen minutes late, could you put something on for me?' I put this record on and I forgot to move the thing from 45 to 33 RPM. So I was playing this 35-minute jazz thing at the wrong speed. Radio then was a little bit renegade and kind of wild and fun. I think it probably still is, but it might just be in pockets. Then again, you have to understand that radio had to go through the '80s, which was a pretty rough decade to come out of without a few shivers."

Chronic Town was released on August 24, 1982, shortly after the band signed with I.R.S. (leaving David Healey's aptly named Dasht Hopes label in the dust). The record fared well both on the college radio charts (where it took up residence in the Top Five) and at the record stores, where it sold a surprising—for a relatively unknown band on a small label—20,000 copies its first year. Favorable press certainly didn't hurt, especially the Village

Voice's prestigious year-end Pazz & Jop Poll—the cumulative vote of most of the nation's top rock critics—which rated the EP second best for the year.

Throughout 1982, R.E.M. crisscrossed America in support of *Chronic Town,* playing every tacky disco and Steak and Brew with a new wave night that would have the band. In the course of its travels, the band noticed that the names of some other bands would always keep popping up—Husker Du, the Replacements, the Neats, Black Flag. It began to get an idea that it wasn't alone in its dedication to the road—that there were fellow travelers out there.

"I think that between us and Black Flag," remembers Peter Buck, "we were very involved, the two of us, kind of—I hate to say blazing a path—linking up. You find out there's a pizza parlor in Charlotte you can play at or a biker bar some place in Rolling Rock, North Carolina, or something. We'd play, and I know that Black Flag would play because there were always posters. Other bands would call us and we'd say, "Yeah, you can play this place. It's all right. The guy is nice." A lot of places we played, we were the first out-of-town band ever to play there. It was all local bands. So whatever the local scene was was just thirteen people went out to the show and most of them were probably in bands."

What drove you guys to do that?
Buck: Once you're playing, it seems a whole lot better than working. I could go back and be a janitor or work at the newspaper or at the record store, or we could go on tour. And who in their right mind wouldn't want to go on tour? You know, playing in a cool rock band.

Oh, of course it was a drag, too, you know. You'd go weeks without bathing. We used to put lemon juice in our hair because lemon juice cleans your hair out. If you just run it through. It makes it stick up really cool, too. But if you don't have a chance to wash your hair, especially if your hair is short, just put lemon juice in it. It cleans it right up. It makes it feel like straw.

We didn't really eat anything. We slept on people's floors. It was kind of romantic. It was cool. I guess a lot of people who weren't ambitious, weren't directed as we were, might've found it too much. I know that even people who were three years older than us were just local band heroes, were just like, "We're not gonna tour. Fuck that. We'll go to New York, that's it." They'd always be like, "Well, who wants to go to the Midwest?" Which is a good enough question.

Did you make money out there? Were there points when you said, Why do we bother?

We never lost money on a tour. But, then again, we didn't get per diems and stuff. As long as we got money for gas to the next place....Because you can just keep doing that. Everyone that we talked to, like the people in Pylon, said, "Why in the world do you go out there and break your ass for virtually no money?" Whereas I had trouble understanding why they would want to work a day job. It's not like these jobs are great. Wouldn't you rather sleep late and play at night and get free drinks and get to see the country than work at the paint store or whatever? It seemed to make sense. To us, the doing it was its own reward. It wasn't necessarily because—

You weren't going for any gold—like trying to sell more records. The maxim about R.E.M. is that the reason you got successful when other bands didn't was because you toured so much.

In a way, it's true. You could see it kind of growing. We were always popular in Athens. The first date we ever charged money, there were five hundred people at it. We've always been popular here. It's kind of luck to have these people see us when they hadn't seen other bands. But, it was the same in other towns. We'd go to towns and there'd be twenty people the first night, and they'd all talk to us. We'd go back three months later or a month

later and there'd be eighty. Every single place we ever went it grew like that. So we would go, "Well, we must be okay." And we'd always go, "Now we're popular in Atlanta and Athens, and we're also popular in Nashville and Memphis and North Carolina and South Carolina." Every time we toured, we tried to put in one new territory. "Well, we haven't been to New Orleans yet. Let's see if we can go down there and get popular." Because we could do it more.

The constant touring helped ensure two things: 1) that the band would be tight as glue when they went back into the recording studio, and 2) that when the next record came out, the audience for it would be that much larger. People all over the country had heard of R.E.M. now, through a combination of good press and constant road work. Even if it was only, as Peter says, "thirteen people in each town," there are a lot of towns in America.

When it came time to record *Murmur*, R.E.M.'s

Above: R.E.M. at Walter's Bar-B-Q, legendary local pig-out joint for which the band later recorded an inebriated promo song (included on the Dead Letter Office *compilation).*

Right: Peter Buck: [On early tours] we didn't really eat anything. We slept on people's floors. It was kind of romantic. It was cool.

```
r.e.m.
P.o. box 8032
aTHens, Ga  30603
```

☐ RRRRRR
☐ MY THROAT HURTS.
☐ I CAN.
☐ A MIGHTY BIG WORD.
☐ BURY MAGNETS.
SWALLOW THE RAPTURE.

MAMMOTH HUGE COLOSSAL UNDERSTATED

first full-length LP, R.E.M.'s record company first suggested the band try a different producer. After all, *Chronic Town* had been recorded before the boys were even under contract and presented to the label as a fait accompli (one which, of course, I.R.S. was more than happy to release). But for the full-length album—in essence, the band's official "debut"—label president Jay Boberg thought they could benefit from a more professional guiding hand.

Always ready to try anything, R.E.M. went to Atlanta to record a version of "Catapult" with then-unknown British producer Stephen Hague, who would later make a name for himself producing the Pet Shop Boys and New Order. The experience proved near disastrous, as Hague put them through such unfamiliar (albeit standard practice for the industry) paces as recording with a metronomic "click" track and forcing them to record numerous takes of the same song. Hague then took the tapes and overdubbed synthesizer parts onto them himself, to the great dismay of the band, who then told I.R.S. in no uncertain terms that it wanted to work with Mitch Easter again.

I.R.S. readily complied after hearing a demo of "Pilgrimage" recorded by Easter and hastily enlisted friend Don Dixon at Reflection Studios in Charlotte. (Easter's own Drive-In Studio was considered too low-tech for the job.) And in early 1983, the band went to work on *Murmur*, this time with producers who were fully in tune with R.E.M.'s iconoclastic way of working and who saw the band's stylistic quirks as the innovations they were rather than impediments to making a "commercial" album. Once again, the band felt free to experiment with new sounds and new ways of recording (for instance, Michael Stipe recorded in a stairway out of sight of the mixing desk), and was indulged by Easter's and Dixon's mutual sense

Above: Another fan club postcard, featuring a typically Stipean bout of word-fever. Michael's intense work habits resulted in a massive output of sometimes unfathomable artifacts such as this.

Right: At RFK stadium in 1983. Michael Stipe: "Looking at someone through their creative output is a blurred vision, but it really can be a very beautiful one."

that even if what the band was doing didn't follow the established rules of recording, or at least of recording a pop album, whatever it was doing seemed to work. Which was the important thing.

Murmur will forever carry a weight unequal to the other records in the R.E.M. catalog, simply because it was the first—or at least, the first most people would hear of the band. The album was an *event*, in a way that nothing afterward could ever be. It was the opening salvo in a fight to regain some of the credibility for American "underground," or less commercial, bands currently held by the predominantly British crop of new wave bands, many of whom were synth-heavy and more concerned with fashion than music. The Brits had taken over leadership in the new-music field with the advent of the Sex Pistols in 1976; ever since then, with the notable exception of some of the New York punk and new wave groups, tastemakers had looked to the U.K. for the latest in musical innovation. The plain fact was, though, that most of the music coming from there completely sucked and that the tunnel vision with which critics regarded the American music scene caused some quite excellent groups to be ignored. With the success of *Murmur*, all that gradually changed over the next few years, to the point where in 1986 or so, American indie rock reigned supreme even in the British music press. The tables had been turned, and R.E.M. did a large share of the

turning—not just by releasing good albums but by tirelessly promoting American rock on any of their fairly frequent jaunts through Europe and in any interviews they held with the European (especially British) press. At first, the band's claims that, far from an isolated instance, R.E.M. was just one of a number of great bands (it would point to the Replacements, Hüsker Dü, Black Flag, among others) establishing themselves on the fringe of the American music industry, were met with disbelief. But time would prove the band right.

For these reasons, though, *Murmur* has often been unjustly over- and underrated—because of what it represents rather than what it is, which is just another really good record by a really good band. Coming out when it did, in 1983, when the dominant sound on the charts was Eurythmics- and Police-oriented, it sounded much more abrasive and revolutionary than it does today, but the truth is that *Murmur* was far from the most abrasive music being produced at the time. Hell, the record's almost a pop album.

Every good rock 'n' roll band needs an anthem, and for a long time, "Radio Free Europe" was R.E.M.'s anthem. *Murmur*'s rerecorded version of the band's very first single (R.E.M. bought the rights to the song, as well as its B side, "Sitting Still," back from Johnny Hibbert for the retrospectively paltry sum of $2,000) begins with an

eerily spacey intro, then slams into the closest thing to a rock song the band would record for some time. Michael Stipe's ambiguously rousing lyrics ("Put that, put that, put that on your wall / That this isn't country at all") have been variously interpreted to be about everything from the sorry state of pop radio to the situation in Eastern Europe. Personally, I've always liked to think they were about his cat.

"Pilgrimage" fades in gracefully after the chiming bell-like ending to "Radio," its layers of backing vocals lending it an almost gospel, elegiac quality. "Rest assured this will not last / Take a turn for the worse" croons Stipe cheerily; in general, the song's lyrics are clearly and unmistakably enunciated, which leads one to wonder where people got the idea that you couldn't tell what Stipe was saying (this was the album, after all, that cynics nicknamed *Mumble*). Next is "Laughing," whose vocals have a vaguely sinister tone undercut by the strangely light-hearted arrangement—stacks of acoustic guitars piled on an intriguing bass-and-drums-only intro. This particular song does feature a rather mush-mouthed performance by Stipe, although certain catchphrases ("Martyred, misconstrued") do manage to poke through the murk. The way the arrangement builds from the intro on to the end, adding a sound here and there, pulling back when necessary, provides a good example of how developed the band's sense of dynamics was even at this early stage in its development. Rather than just bashing through the song on one level, the band provides definite peaks and valleys to pull the listener in and then sucker-punch him when he's lulled by a quiet moment or a pretty melody. It's a trick many bands never learn.

"Talk About the Passion," the next song, enters with a strong, suggestive guitar line that basically carries the weight of the rest of the song ("Not everyone can carry the weight of the world," sings Stipe, but apparently Peter Buck's Rickenbacker can). The band then adds a low, throaty cello part to the arrangement which helps hold things together and adds to the baroque mood of the lyrics, which may or may not be, again, about Stipe's cat. "Moral Kiosk" surfs in next on a fast-paced, stuttering riff, then lurches into a sparse, almost Gang of Four-ish arrangement (betraying, possibly, the influence of Athens compatriots Pylon) before reaching the intriguing chanted chorus. This song is about the effects of feeding spaghetti to one's cat too early in the day.

"Perfect Circle" is the first real "ballad" the band ever recorded; it remains among its finest work. Its simple guitar- and piano-based arrangement is quietly majestic, and Stipe's clearly enunciated but nonlinear lyrics serve to heighten rather than to detract from the obviously emotional content of the song. His phrasing, on "Perfect Circle" especially, but on the album in general as well, is remarkably assured for such an undeveloped voice; because of it he can get away with an occasional slurred phrase or weak lyric. The next song, "Catapult," used to open the second side of the record, back when there were records. Its haphazard position on the CD only emphasizes what a silly little pop song it is. "Did we miss anything?" Stipe asks in the course of it, which is either a reference to the early, alcohol-sodden days of the Athens scene or another obscure feline reference.

The B side of the Hib-Tone single was "Sitting Still"; listening to the rerecorded version here, it doesn't sound much like a B side. The song is an example of the type of R.E.M. arrangement where Stipe's voice would be used pretty strictly as simply an additional instrument. The lyrics are deliberately stretched and slurred so that verbal sense doesn't interfere with the purely musical value of the syllables. "Sitting" features a deceptively inventive bass line and some of Buck's more propulsive rhythm playing. "I can hear you, can you hear me" at the end of the song must be one of the more deliberately ironic lines Stipe's written.

Above: R.E.M. Christmas card. As the band looked ahead to 1984, things certainly seemed to be falling into place.

Right: Michael Stipe: "There's all this stuff that goes around about me and most of it's not true."

Much has been made of how, supposedly, the song "9-9" was purposefully recorded so that the only words one can make out are "conversation fear," which is what the song's ostensibly about; and while there's certainly a deliberately buried spoken-word intro and break, you can make out a lot of the rest of the words. The explanation was probably another of Stipe's famous put-ons. The music is the most dissonant on the record, and again sounds strongly reminiscent of the Gang of Four's minimalist, rhythmic style.

"Shaking Through" begins with a Pete Townshend-like series of suspended chords before launching into one of the prettier melodies on the record, especially in the chorus (even if Michael sings it a little off-key in the chorus). "Autumn marches on, yellow like a geisha doll," he croons—one of the more affecting lyrical images on *Murmur*. "We Walk" follows, a pedestrian (in more ways than one), country-inflected ditty, and the album closes with "West of the Fields," which feels like a throwaway track, saved by the moody break with rattling chains, and an eerie organ "outro" to complement the eerie "Radio Free Europe" intro.

Possibly the most striking feature of *Murmur* is its inventiveness. Despite the somewhat limited stylistic range the band possessed at this early stage in its career, it never seemed to run out of ways to make a song interesting, whether it be a trick of arrangement or an unexpected sound half-buried in the mix. One of the record's most persistent delights is in the relistening; almost always, something new, something you hadn't heard before, yields itself. That this sophistication is the product of a near-neophyte outfit is astonishing enough; that it took them only about three weeks to complete the record is well-nigh unbelievable.

Shortly after *Murmur*'s debut, Michael Stipe began to be plagued with the "mystic young poet" tag that would follow him for the rest of his career—a tag in part accentuated by the undeniably eccentric bent to his personality, at times, but which for the most part remains undeserved.

The guy's certainly intense about his work, but no more so than, say, a really good plumber would be. He believes in what he's doing, in the value of his music and in the uses to which he can put his celebrity. But the adoration of his so-called "distipeles" and the loathing of his detractors has resulted in a sometimes distorted view of his character, a situation not helped by Stipe's renowned reclusiveness.

"There's only a certain degree to which someone who doesn't actually know you can understand you," comments Michael. "The information you get about any kind of artist's personality from his or her work may be conflicting within itself, but it does tend to point toward what this person is about. This is their aesthetic. This is what they appreciate. Looking at someone through their creative output is a blurred vision, but it really can be a very beautiful one. I just don't think that it gets you closer to what that person is truly about.

"There's all this stuff that goes around about me and most of it's not true. Or blown out of proportion. That just comes with the celebrity thing. I think Faulkner got it. People in his town called him Count No Count because he walked around with a high collar. Simply because he enjoyed it. What a wack. Eccentricity is an easy face to put on, because you can get away with anything. There's a history of people who spend the last half of their lives trying to debunk their celebrated eccentric tag and convince people how normal they are. I certainly don't want to fall into that. Ultimately, I don't give a shit what people think about me. It's probably a modern phenomenon that one has to know so much about the creator of something. It's all pretty one-dimensional and single-faceted, and I think that maybe really smart people like Madonna who really want to climb the ladder can latch onto one thing, change it a lot, but basically remain the same. Her thing, of course, is sex and power, and it obviously works."

Whatever Stipe's *thing* is, it, too, obviously works. And in 1983, people were just beginning to realize that.

C H A P T E R   3

T H E   M I D D L E   A G E S
1 9 8 4 – 1 9 8 9

THE MIDDLE AGES

The release of *Murmur* marked in a pretty definite way the end of the "old" Athens scene. R.E.M. wasn't even in town very much anymore—the band was more or less constantly touring, promoting its new album. And of the old-line bands that were still in town, only Love Tractor had any real staying power, any real desire to follow in R.E.M.'s tire tracks. No one else had ever been in it to win it. No one else seemed to care the necessary much. Until, that is, word began to spread that Athens looked good on a band's résumé, and increased the chances that "Joe A&R Man" at "MegaBig Records" would seriously listen to your demo tape. The scene rapidly turned more and more careerist. Bands such as Buzz of Delight (fea-

turing a self-confessed social climber from Lincoln, Nebraska, Matthew Sweet) formed with the sole intent of moving to Athens and climbing on the backs of R.E.M. (and then getting out as soon as they got a record deal), started cropping up. Buzz of Delight was even featured in *The Athens Show* in early 1984, a video presentation of Pylon's farewell performance (at which Love Tractor also played), thought by some to mark the first formal attempt by local promoters to "cash in" on the growing perception of Athens as a hotbed of new music.

It's hard to blame the good people of Athens for thinking they had got hold of something special. And harder still to expect them to keep their heads when the mainstream press began billowing down in scads, bringing back to the big cities tales of the wonder of Athens rock—everyone from *Newsweek* to the *Washington Post* to (my personal favorite) *Entertainment Tonight*. Despite the efforts of longtime scenesters to quell the rising hysteria (i.e., protect the "purity of essence" of their long-cherished scene) and their disgust at the naked ambition of some of the newcomers, Athens soon gathered a reputation as a mecca for the non-new wave underground rock sprouting like peach fuzz all over the country, especially in the South, in the wake of R.E.M.'s success. Most of these bands were way more pop-oriented than the first wave of the Athens scene, which further added to the disgruntlement of old-timers, who never had quite cottoned to R.E.M.'s hybrid jangle. And, truth to tell, most of the bands who moved to Athens with careerist motives were pretty much worthless. They attracted a certain amount of record company and media attention, but sooner or later faded into obscurity, the "sooner" usually depending on whether or not they were

AFTER SHOW ONLY

produced by (or enjoyed the sponsorship of) a member of R.E.M. It's a process that continues today.

R.E.M.'s live show at this particular juncture in its performing career was still a singularly kinetic experience. Michael Stipe's manic dancing and

Above: With success comes responsibility. As their career progressed, R.E.M.'s tours became more thoroughly planned and professional. As well as shorter.

Right: R.E.M.'s live performances would change over the middle years, as Michael Stipe grew more sedate and less willing to "perform" for the audience.

posturing, clinging to the microphone in imitation, you'd have to believe, of uncontrollable passion (kind of an art-school version of Steve Martin's happy feet), was naturally the center of attention, but the other band members were no slouches either when it came to rock moves. Peter Buck would prowl and twirl around the stage with an antic Keith Richards/mellow Pete Townshend hybrid attitude, while Mike Mills would occasionally leap in the air like one of the guys from the Jam. While these days, the band's audiences were growing to the point where no matter how isolated the town R.E.M. played, a decent crowd would show, there were still off nights, when attendance was sparse. It didn't matter to the band, whose attitude was that even if only 30 people came, those 30 people would see the best rock show of their lives and go tell their friends, so that the next time through town there'd be a hundred people, and so on. So that the level of energy R.E.M. devoted to each show, with rare exceptions, was the limit to which they physically had access. Which, as devoted concert-goers will doubtless already know, is an uncommon attribute among touring bands.

R.E.M.'s performance would change over the year, as Stipe grew more sedate and less willing to "perform" for the audience in the ascending period of the band's career. It would change again when the band made its transformation from cult item to arena headliner, as Stipe would come to terms with his duties as a performer and attempt to redefine the way an arena band can present itself—selling to the audience without selling out.

But that was much later. In 1984, after an extensive round of touring, the quartet returned to North Carolina and the comforts of Mitch Easter

and Don Dixon's Reflection Studios to record the "eagerly awaited" follow-up to *Murmur*. The somewhat sardonically titled second LP, *Reckoning*, was very much a road record in the sense that the songs had all survived trial by fire on the road, some of them had been written there, and the stripped-down arrangements reflected more accurately the live band's sound at that time. The band spent very little time recording *Reckoning*—somewhere between 11 and 25 days, depending on who you ask, which is still infinitesimal by big-league standards—concentrating quite deliberately on capturing the essence of the songs rather than presenting them through layers of sound as on *Murmur*. The result is, in many ways, a better record than *Murmur*—overall, the songs are more substantial, depending less on elaboration to get over than on pure, emotive playing. Stipe's singing is improved (not in the "more decipherable" sense, but in the "on key" sense), and while Peter Buck's pocketful of guitar tricks is no deeper (and in fact would never get deeper), his mastery of those tricks is greater, his ability to come up with, say, just the right single note solo ("Camera") fairly unequaled, both at the time and in the years to come.

"Harborcoat," really a cut-and-paste job combining alternate parts of the same song, begins the record in typically art school fashion; but it's significant that the band chose to start off its sophomore effort not with a "Radio Free Europe"-like bang but with a relative whimper. The next song, "7 Chinese Brothers," benefits from Buck's two-string droning intro (he'd use that trick a lot on the record) and a concise, catchy chorus. "So. Central Rain" and "Pretty Persuasion," the next two songs, are really the highlight of the record. The former is a relaxed, folky pop song whose repeated refrain of "I'm sorry" lends it a slightly melancholic air, while the latter's rousing arpeggiated intro crashes into as anthemic a structure as the band would ever record.

Nevertheless, the best song on *Reckoning* might be one of the most overlooked: "Second Guessing," a streamlined rockish little number clocking in at under three minutes (the shortest song on the album) that benefits from seamless

---

Above: "Fall On Me," the first single from Reconstruction, *remains one of the best-constructed R.E.M. songs ever.*

Right: For most of 1984, the key word was "Work." The band played nearly a hundred shows world-wide and involved themselves in a number of side projects.

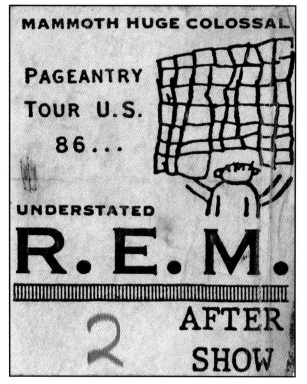

construction, wickedly propulsive guitar playing, and a lyric simplicity and clarity clamps hold of the listener. Whether the song's meaning has anything to do with perceived reactions to the band's music, or a kind of arrogant R.E.M. attitude ("here we are"), seems dubious, but taken that way, the song bites a little harder. "(Don't Go Back to) Rockville," drastically slowed down from its early, thrashier incarnation, and recorded pretty much in one take as a favor to Bertis Downs, who was a big fan of the song, turned out to be a cultish classic. The song was written by Mike Mills as a plea to a friend who was planning to move out of town; its unusually straightforward lyrics benefit from Stipe's near-camp country delivery. The rote R.E.M.-isms of "Little America" are redeemed (somewhat) by the song's roguish references to manager Jefferson Holt's navigational abilities ("Jefferson, I think we're lost"), and by its mini travelogue ("Another Greenville, another Magic Mart").

Holt and partner Bertis Downs had over the past couple of years gradually assumed more and more responsibility for the running of R.E.M.'s business affairs. By the release of *Reckoning* they had become indispensable to the operation of the band's day-to-day affairs—to the point where they have often been credited as band members on subsequent album sleeves. Holt and Downs's casual, easy-going style of management well-suited the band's tone, and helped further to define them. Where other groups might have considered near-

suicidal Holt's decision to maintain Athens as base of operations (nearly everyone else in the industry was based in either New York or Los Angeles), R.E.M. realized that there wasn't any good reason to have an office anywhere else. Part of this decision was due to the band's long-term commitment to the city of Athens and to its friends there, and part was just plain good business sense. Everything in Athens was cheaper; the only downside to the band's remaining there was that its phone bills were bigger.

Reckoning's reception proved somewhat better than expected, certainly dispelling fears of any sort of sophomore jinx. It reached the Top 30 on the American pop charts, a more than respectable showing for a supposedly "underground" band. And while the critical reception wasn't as unanimously extravagant as that for *Murmur*, few reviews pegged the record as a disappointment. (Typical reactions ranged from "You can hear the lyrics better"—untrue—to "Less guitar heavy," sort of untrue.)

For the rest of the year, the key word was work. The band played nearly a hundred shows worldwide, and, as if that weren't enough, even started playing in side projects, as well as making guest appearances on friends' records. Perhaps the most notable of these side projects was the debut of the Hindu Love Gods, fronted by local Athenian and longtime friend Bryan Cook. The Love Gods, featuring R.E.M. minus Stipe, were intended as more or less a glorified bar band, and played mostly covers mixed with some early R.E.M. songs that the band had subsequently dropped from its set—making its set list a fairly close replica of the "early R.E.M. experience," with the obvious difference that instead of the lithe, diminutive Stipe as front man, audience members were treated to the sight of the rather, um, bigger Cook.

The band also took part helping out legendary singer-songwriter Warren Zevon with his *Sentimental Hygiene* album; its assistance helped in part to resuscitate the performer's failing career. During the recording of demos for *Sentimental Hygiene*, the Hindu Love Gods decided to record a single, with Zevon helping out on keyboards, as well as play a live gig in Athens at the 40 Watt.

Above: Life's Rich Pageant *represented in many critics' minds a return to form after the spotty, unusually somber* Fables of the Reconstruction.

Right: Stipe eventually emerged from his performing shell and began developing new, more theatrical ways to project his several personas to the cheap seats.

Later, during the sessions for *Sentimental Hygiene*, the Love Gods would spend an evening recording a short set of covers that would come back to haunt them when Zevon's record company decided to release them as an album in 1990.

"We did that record literally in about the time it takes to listen to it," recalls Bill Berry. "We all went to dinner and I guess some of us got more plowed than we should have, and we came back and just had fun in the studio. I think it's really great, but unfortunately there's a whole side to it that's very black and ugly.

"Basically we were exploited. We love Warren and don't regret doing it at all, but his management and the record company kept begging us to support it with publicity and a tour or something. But we can't just drop what we're doing. It was just one fun drunken night long ago. We refused to appear in the video, and now they have a version with our heads cut off. I mean, we hardly even appear in our own videos."

Despite slight mishaps of that nature, the band closed out the year as leading lights of the American underground, however loosely defined, and as a rapidly growing influence for scores of sharp-minded, young, guitar-playing rascals. As the group got ready to begin work on its third LP, college rock was in full swing. The last thing, then, the real R.E.M. wanted to do was to make another record that sounded like R.E.M.

So it didn't. R.E.M. went to London, enlisting

the services of veteran folk-rock producer Joe Boyd, who had worked with the seminal folk rock band Fairport Convention in the late '60s. As much for a change of scene as for a change of sound, the decision to record elsewhere proved fraught with tension, as the band clashed with a producer not used to dealing with a band so adamantly sure of its artistic self. Gloomy, fog-ridden England helped little to foster good feeling among the band members, who moreover were feeling the strain of a seemingly unending (if self-inflicted) work schedule. Put plainly, R.E.M. was not having a good time, and the band had, heretofore, always been about having a good time.

The result, *Fables of the Reconstruction* (or *Reconstruction of the Fables*, as the title can alternately be read), is a dark, slightly fractured album. But that said, almost all R.E.M. albums have a dark, slightly fractured feel to them, and there's much on *Reconstruction* to recommend it, even if Michael Stipe's recent assertion that it's now his

Above: Document *was in some ways R.E.M.'s hard-rockiest album to date, thought the "Work" tour was, ironically, its shortest ever.*

Right: After completing Document*, the band also completed its recording deal with I.R.S., which left it free to negotiate a monstrously lucrative pact with Warner Bros.*

HO,HO,HO WE REAllY HAVE SOMETHING TO BE MERRY ABOUT - CARL GRASSO AGREEd to RELEASE tHE HINDU LOVE,(BRIAN COCKE, PETER BUCK, MIKE MILLS, & BILL BERRY), GODS SINGLE. ((REAd THE LETTER BELOW)).

R.E.M, et al -
Help! I can't take it anymore!
I'm drowning in Hindu Love
God fan letters. I give in!
I'll do it! We'll do it!
Please, we'll release the
record...Just make it stop!!
Whatever you want!!! 8-color love,
limos, full page ad in LIFE magazine!
Anything! JUST MAKE THEM STOP!!

Love,
CARL

I.R.S.

LET'S MAKE A NEW YEAR'S RESOLUTION - IF WE don't SEE tHIS RECORD IN EARLY FEBRUARY THEN CARL GRASSO GETS A NEW POOL OF LETTERS!! •

"favorite album" smacks more than a little of typical Stipean, uh, bullshit. The record does have the distinction of containing the one truly awful R.E.M. song ever officially released: "Can't Get There From Here"'s appallingly lead-footed stab at, I guess, James Brown-style funk could not have been redeemed by any amount of vocal or guitar overdubbing. Other than that, though, "Driver 8," "Maps and Legends," and especially "Green Grow the Rushes" are all prime R.E.M. material and continue to be a standard part of the band's repertoire.

Fables is also notable because it contains the first furtive steps of Stipe's eventual transformation into a political, or at least politicized, lyric writer—most apparently on "Green Grow the Rushes." It's also the first record after which the band began to be accused—on any significant scale, at least—of "selling out."

"I understand that," says Michael Stipe. "I remember when Blondie did 'Heart of Glass,' I said, 'Sold out, see ya. I'm moving back to the Slits,' or whatever, and when Gang of Four put out *Hard*, I was like, 'Oh fuck, here we go!' I listen to that record now, and it's amazing. When something that's considered secret and wonderful is revealed to the world, it becomes a little less wonderful. It's time to find something new. That's a legitimate and healthy cycle."

The cries from wounded fans stemmed less from the content of the album than from the simple fact that, despite a critical reception that could (for once) accurately be called "mixed," *Fables* was selling better and faster than any of its predecessors. As a result, R.E.M. was forced to play bigger theaters to accommodate its growing legion of fans. As a result, the band was perceived as having left behind the fans who nurtured it through its nascence. The fact that R.E.M. had done so with little obvious compromise in terms of artistic integrity mattered little to the angry faithful. Their main complaint with R.E.M. was that the band had become successful. That wasn't supposed to happen.

In any event, after a fair measure of soul-searching and even fairer measure of renewed touring, R.E.M. decided to do what it had been accused of doing the record before: It decided to sell out. Actually, what the band really decided to do was to make a more straight-ahead, big-sounding rock record with enormous-sounding drums and more distinct vocals, but in doing so, it knew that the result would have an easier time of it out in the world of mainstream pop. At least, that was the idea. But the band wasn't about to change its songwriting style in any way or by doing anything else to compromise itself.

Accordingly, R.E.M. chose Don Gehman to produce the next record. Gehman was known primarily for his well-regarded work with John Mellencamp, and initially wasn't real hot on the idea of producing a record by such determined iconoclasts. Gehman liked making hit records, and he wasn't at all sure R.E.M. were capable of (or interested in) making hit records. But a meeting of the two parties took place at which Gehman's fears were largely dissuaded, and a demo of a new song, "Fall on Me," came out well enough to convince all concerned that the right choice had been made. In early 1986, the group began work on the archly titled *Life's Rich Pageant* (the title taken from a line made famous by Peter Sellers's Inspector Clouseau character in the popular Pink Panther movies).

The year 1986 also saw the official canonization

Above: From a fan club mailing announcing the release of the first Hindu Love Gods single. Side projects have always been a way of life for R.E.M.

Right: Former dB Peter Holsapple (left of Peter Buck) accompanied the band on 1989's Green *tour, and played a considerable amount of guitar on* Out of Time.

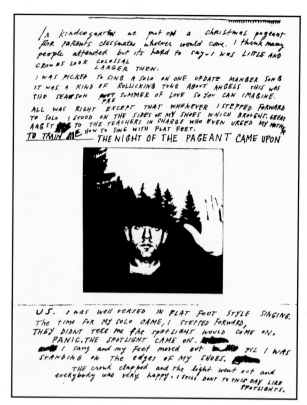

of the Athens scene in the form of the documentary *Athens Inside/Out*, which most longtime scenesters viewed, pretty much rightly so, as a farce. Although the members of R.E.M. were, justifiably, featured performers, other artists covered included the Flat Duo Jets, who had just moved to town a couple of months previously, and folk painter Howard Finster, who didn't live in Athens and whose relevance to the scene was limited to Michael Stipe's infatuation with folk art. The fact was, whatever "scene" the cameras managed to document, it bore little resemblance to the magical confluence of personality and happenstance that had made the original scene so special. Athenian rock in 1986 was a pretty ugly thing.

Of course, and as always, there was R.E.M. Cloistered in Indiana while working on *Life's Rich Pageant*, the band saw through an explosion of creativity—in large part out of necessity, as few songs for the new record were finished—that resulted in its most articulate work to date. Pageant's highlight was "Fall on Me," in this writer's opinion still the best song the band's ever written (it beats out "Losing My Religion" by a notch), and by any standards an evanescent slice of pop. The songs bear witness to a further development in overtly political lyric writing by Stipe, especially on "The Flowers of Guatemala" and "Cuyahoga." "Fall on Me," too, has been interpreted by many as a warning against acid rain, but sounds too personal to be so simply construed. Occasionally, the new

clarity in Stipe's lyrics reveals, just as many (including their author himself, probably) had feared, a tendency toward occasional heavy-handedness. "We are young despite the years / We are concern / We are hope despite the times" he sings in "These Days," while many listeners became sick despite the antacid.

Once again, the record outsold its predecessors, becoming the first gold record (denoting sales of at least 500,000) to R.E.M.'s credit. But despite the radio-friendly production and the obvious pop potential of "Fall on Me," the single failed to go higher than 96 on the pop charts (although the album did manage to make it to No. 21). Meanwhile, the band took a much-deserved break from touring for the large part of the year, preferring instead to concentrate on a plethora of side projects—among these the aforementioned work with Warren Zevon on his *Sentimental Hygiene* record—that kept them easily as busy as they might have been if they'd been touring. As usual,

Above: R.E.M. has always maintained one of the best run and genuinely non-exploitative fan clubs in the biz — a model for other alternative bands, like Sonic Youth.

Right: The constant touring brought rumors that some of the band members weren't getting along. As with most such rumors, they turned out to be greatly exaggerated.

> Jefferson's suggestions for making the war more fun.
>
> Buy a billboard and chop out the center - leave the frame.
> Chop down a billboard.
> Use natural products. Boycott Proctor & Gamble.
> Boycott Coors beer.
> Buy stuff from Tom's of Maine. The toothpaste is great.
> Support locally owned businesses - breweries.
> Walk to the nearest river or creek. Follow it until you find the first company that's polluting it and try to make them stop.
> Unplug every T.V. you see.
>
> (Imagine. With all the grain grown to force feed McDonalds cows we could feed the world - imagine - a world full of healthy happy people re creating until there's so many healthy happy people on this teeming planet that little babies fly off the tops of kiddy condos into the ether...!)
>
> Merry Christmas

the R.E.M. work ethic prevailed.

When it came time to record the next album, the band found itself at a crossroads. It had already achieved everything it had ever dared dream in terms of popular acceptance, and the time had come to decide whether to make the effort to put the band over the top to superstardom, or to tone down and tread water, comfortable within the parameters it had so far established. R.E.M.'s record company, I.R.S., desperately wanted the band to commit to a full-scale world-wide tour behind the next album, but the band wasn't entirely sure that I.R.S. had the promotional and distributional wherewithal to make such a tour a worthwhile prospect. Complicating matters was the fact that the next album would be the last of their current contract. After that R.E.M. would be in a position to sign with any label it wanted.

Early in 1987, the band released a collection of B sides and unreleased songs called *Dead Letter Office*, partly as a way of stemming the rising tide of bootlegged R.E.M. material. Puckish liner notes by Peter Buck helped bolster a collection that was pretty much rough going. For all R.E.M.'s vaunted tradition of covers, the band doesn't pull off versions of other people's songs very well most of the time. Everything it does sounds just too damn much like R.E.M., which in almost any other context is an unmixed blessing. In the context of a cover song, it just makes the band sound like R.E.M. playing someone else's song—which just isn't that much fun. The other

obscurities on this record pretty much deserve to stay that way.

Diversionary releases aside, work on the next record now beckoned. When Don Gehman recommended Scott Litt to the band for a one-off project in late 1986, R.E.M. found his modus operandi so conducive to its own that the band asked him to help produce its next effort (from now on, all R.E.M. records would be coproductions with the band). Litt picked Nashville to record what was to become *Document*, widely considered the group's "breakthrough" album.

Which in a sense it was. With the release of *Document* in the fall of 1987, R.E.M. effectively brought about the death of college rock—at least of the college rock it had helped foster. When *Document* went platinum (denoting sales of at least 1,000,000), the band had grown to the point where it could no longer serve as a hip influence. It had become, instead, a target for the hip—it now became an insult in collegiate ranks to be found with a trace of R.E.M.'s influence in your sound. Which, considering the plethora of truly bad bands who followed in R.E.M.'s musical footsteps, was not an entirely unfavorable development at all.

Document was easily the biggest, boldest record R.E.M. had made to date. Michael Stipe's lyrics were now not only mixed up and clearly enunciated at (almost) all times, a lot of the time you could *actually understand what he was saying.* Which didn't stop people from misunderstanding him anyway. The most notorious example of this is, of course, the first single, and R.E.M.'s first top ten hit, "The One I Love." An unmitigatedly vicious song whose lyrics are an obvious brush-off to whomever their object might be, most Americans listened only to the first two lines ("This one goes out to the one I love / This one goes out to the one I left behind") and the soaring music and pegged it as a sweet love song. Well, we should all be misunderstood with such lucrative results. Other highlights of the album include the classic Dylanesque word-barrage of "It's the End of the World as We Know It (And I Feel Fine)" and the driving rocker "Finest Worksong," which is as succinct a summation as any of the dominant

---

Above: Manager Jefferson Holt's eco-friendly advice. R.E.M. have always been very active environmental supporters.

Right: The end of 1989 found the band looking forward to perhaps its most ambitious world-wide tour ever, in support of Green.

R.E.M. ethic.

The success of *Document* only underscored the choice R.E.M. would now be faced to make—whether to re-sign with I.R.S. or to move on to a label with more resources. Ultimately, they chose to move on, signing with Warner Brothers for an undisclosed but undoubtedly enormous sum—although the group maintained that it wasn't the money that finally persuaded it, but Warner Brothers's enormous international distribution and promotion network that would enable the band to reach the worldwide audience it had never managed to cultivate thus far in its career.

R.E.M., therefore, began work on the follow-up to *Document* with the security of a long-term contract and the determination that with this next album it would finally make the big push to the next level of success. Scott Litt was once again chosen to coproduce, but the band's declared aim was to make the new album a stylistic departure from what it perceived as the slightly stale format of the last two records. What it ended up with was *Green*.

The album's title reflected the culmination of Michael Stipe's—and the band's as a whole—politicization. Stipe had been for some time now increasingly involved in a variety of (usually environmentally tinged) extramusical political causes, and *Green*, in the sense of "concerned with the environment" (e.g., Germany's Green Party), fit the tenor of the new record perfectly. *Green* was the first record to actually print the lyrics to an R.E.M. song: The song was "World Leader Pretend," whose thematic importance to the "mes-

sage" of the album was thus underscored, as ambiguous as even those black-and-white lyrics might have been. "I've a rich understanding of my finest defenses," he sings, but whether in character or from the heart it's impossible to know.

Musically, *Green* ranges from the simplistic ("Stand") to the stomping, almost garish ("Orange Crush") to the oblique ("Hairshirt"). It's not the best R.E.M. album, and it's not the worst. Neither is it the stylistic departure the band had hoped for—that would come with the next album. But it does have the distinction of possibly being the album R.E.M. toured the hardest behind. The band would hit the road shortly after the release of *Green* for a nine-month world tour—the tour I.R.S. had wanted the band to do for *Document*. And the band did it all without the benefit of the seemingly ubiquitous specter of corporate sponsorship, turning down possibly millions of dollars in the process.

"We turn down most of the commercial stuff. It's horrid," comments Mike Mills. "You can tell Eric Clapton, Phil Collins, Steve Winwood, and Pete Townshend they can shove it. Corporate sponsorship is the way of the world, and it's futile to fight it, but I don't have to like it. All the old science fiction novels used to say corporations

would take over everything in the future. Now it's true. I don't care what bands say. 'Oh, we can't tour without corporate sponsorship.' I'm here to tell you that's bullshit."

The constant touring also brought rumors that some of the band members weren't getting along; specifically, that Michael Stipe couldn't stand the presence of his fellow band mates so much so that he insisted on traveling in a separate tour bus.

Peter Buck dispels the unfounded gossip.

"We have two buses," he explains. "Usually me and Bill and Mike ride on the noisy bus, and Jefferson, Bert, and Michael ride on the quiet bus. We just divide up those of us who stay up all night on one bus and those of us who go to sleep at one in the morning. Michael has the milk-and-cookies bus. There are actually milk and cookies in his fridge. And on ours, you know, beer and liquor. We'd sit up all night and drink and play records."

Which hardly sounds like a band on the verge of collapse. In truth, the members of R.E.M. seem to enjoy each other's company more than those of most bands of their age and stature. In that respect, they are enormously lucky. In any event, the end of R.E.M.'s tour brought the band to the verge of a new decade with a fistful of great songs and a slew of consistently excellent records. Looking around, there was no other band with R.E.M.'s combination of integrity, ability, concern, and, hell, just plain sense of fun. At the end of one of the worst American decades in recent memory, R.E.M. really was, quite possibly, the country's finest rock'n'roll band.

Which should be worth *something*.

Above: Michael Stipe: "Eccentricity is an easy face to put on, because you can get away with anything. I certainly don't want to fall into that."

R.E.M. AND SPORTS: THE HIDDEN CONNECTION

Sure, they may not look it, but the members of R.E.M. are secretly (with the exception of Michael Stipe, whose sportsmania is limited to word-hurling) major jocks. The following is a rundown of some of their favorite pursuits, as revealed by Peter Buck.

BOWLING

Buck: "Bowling is so, kind of, Archie Bunkerish, but I love it. My grandfather was a semipro bowler. I bowl once a year now. When I was, like, 14, me and my brother were really, really good. For, like, 12-, 13-, 14-year-old kids, we were bowling 180s regularly and stuff. My brother bowled a 216 when he was 12. It was pretty great. He's still got the plaque somewhere at home. We lived in Indiana, you've got to remember, so there's not a lot else to do. That's the reason my grandfather liked me so much, because he was retired. He was playing with older folks. He would always win blue-chip stamps. They had a blue-chip stamp league and he was just a motherfucker. So we'd go over his house and he'd have these shopping carts full of books of blue-chip stamps. My mother would be, like, "We need a couch." And he'd give us 10,000. So I lived off blue-chip stamps all through my childhood. My grandpa liked me because I bowled straight. I never could get a good hook on it. It should go along the gutter and then spin over, like a tornado. I never got the hang of that. So I kind of bowl right down the middle. It works pretty good. I haven't bowled recently much, but I used to be really, really good. If I had kept with it, I'd be pretty good, but I guess you can say that about a lot of stuff.

"Mike and I are within—it depends on the game. Generally, Mike tends to be a little bit better than me at sports things 'cause he actually does them, and I don't. But I'm naturally fairly good. So if we bowl four games, he'll probably beat me three times. Or maybe we'll tie."

PING-PONG

"I never play. Mike plays all the time. I can still beat him now and again. He basically can kick my ass nine times out of ten. Mike is pretty damn good. Mike is really good. When we were working on *Green*, Charlie Sexton was in the studio, too. I had kind of met him over the years. I met him when he was, like, 12. And so we said, 'Hey, Charlie. How're you doing?' And he said, 'Well, there's nothing to do at Bearsville, so we've had these three-month-long Ping-Pong tournaments, and I won. I'm the champ, I got so good at it.' I said, 'Okay, let's play.' And I smoked his ass. I beat him, like, 21 to 6. He was so depressed. I was, like, 'I only played twice the last couple of years. I used to be okay.' And it was, like, I killed him, completely bummed him out."

BADMINTON

"Badminton is fun. I used to have a net over at this other house I lived in. It would be, like, 300 degrees. And you'd go out in the afternoon and whack the ball around until you fell down. Or the birdie or whatever you call it."

CROQUET

"I'm into, believe it or not, croquet now. I got a croquet set for a present. We have these little pool parties. You know, I've got a pool in back of my house. We'll set up the croquet thing and my nephew and all these people totally out of their minds will be like—Well, it's aggressive because you can decide whether you want to score or if you just want to knock someone else out of competition. It's funny, 'cause you always think of people in like straw hats and striped blazers doing it and these very, very British-type people. It's fun. It is aggressive, because you can decide to make one person's life miserable. I kind of like that about the game. It's just, like, no matter if I lose or if I'm in last place, I can make sure that he's below me. It's nice. It's like dodgem cars. You always pick out some helpless kid and just nail him."

R.E.M.

C H A P T E R   4

L O V E   S O N G S ,
N O T H I N G   B U T
L O V E   S O N G S
1 9 9 0 – 1 9 9 1

LOVE SONGS, NOTHING BUT LOVE SONGS

Bill Berry's house, Athens, Georgia, December 1990: R.E.M.'s annual Christmas party is in full swing (formal attire—"It's a good excuse for getting the girls in these great dresses," says Mike Mills). The band has just finished its first record in two years and decided on a name for it: *Out of Time*. Everyone seems in high spirits (or maybe they're just high on spirits)—more than once, Berry has to send out for more alcohol (prompting one wag to suggest the band rename its new album *Out of Beer*). Guests are ushered from room to room and introduced to a number of the Athenian hoi polloi, ranging from Bill's mom to the recently elected mayor (her campaign, we're told, benefited from discreet R.E.M. support). Professional

eccentric Robyn Hitchcock lists aimlessly through the dining room. He's staying at Peter Buck's house while the two work on Robyn's new album (1991's boffo *Perspex Island*). Most of Robyn's days are spent "upstairs in my room, playing guitar quietly, as is my wont," he says.

Michael Stipe walks in fashionably, or maybe just characteristically, late. He's eager to hear people's reaction to the record—many at the party had heard it recently for the first time.

"What'd you think?" Stipe asks at random.

"Um, I like that song 'Sizzling Happy Family,'" replies one poor unfortunate.

"That's 'Shiny Happy People,' " he says, apparently unamused.

"What do you think of it, Michael?" someone else asks.

"I like it now, but I don't know what I'll think of it in a year."

"Do you like it better than *Green?*"

"Yes, much better. That's always the case, though. I always like whatever we've just done. Then you get distance, you get a little bit more objectivity about it and you're able to see the flaws."

Bill Berry passes by. "Hey, Bill, what do you think of the album?" someone asks.

"I don't know," he reflects. "I'm afraid it might be too weird for some people. I'm afraid they might not get it."

Later on, after much more beer has arrived and departed, Peter Buck holds forth in the kitchen on the future of music: "Rock died in 1958, rap in 1983, jazz in—" Peter pauses for a moment.

"Nineteen thirty-nine?" someone suggests.

"Whatever. The point is, the next thing is going to be beyond music. Something where electrical impulses are transmitted directly from the performer to the audience—physically. It'll be like drugs, only better. Like mainlining."

Still later, Michael Stipe muses about the relative success and failure of so many like-styled—and in some cases equally talented—folkish-rock combos,

Above: A succession of successful world tours helped put R.E.M. in the position where they didn't have to tour for Out of Time. *So they didn't.*

Right: In 1991, it became apparent that what had formerly been considered alternative rock had in fact moved into the mainstream.

most of whom sprung up in R.E.M.'s wake. Given the overabundance in the early- to mid-'80s of jangly guitar bands, even if you grant R.E.M. as progenitors, what is it about the band that separates them from the crowd?

"The secret of R.E.M.," says Stipe, clutching a half-empty, half-full glass of vodka, "is that Mike doesn't play bass like a bass player, Peter doesn't play guitar like a guitar player, and I don't sing like a singer. And Bill just sort of holds it all together."

On March 25, 1991, *Out of Time* was loosed upon the world. Almost immediately, it became apparent that the record was not only going to do well, it was going to do better than any previous R.E.M. album—even though the band didn't intend to tour behind it, the strategy that had worked so well with *Green. Out of Time*'s enormous (and unforeseen) success—over three million records sold, three weeks at No. 1 on the *Billboard* pop charts—signaled at once the emergence of R.E.M. as by far the most successful "alternative rock" band (until, that is, Nirvana) and the movement of the alt-rock community as a whole into the mainstream of American music.

In 1991, for the first time, it became clear that what had formerly been considered "alternative" rock—a college-centered marketing group with fairly lucrative, if limited, potential—has in fact moved into the mainstream. This music, which encompasses college rock, rap, thrash, metal, and industrial, and has as many variants as adherents, has slowly attracted a larger and larger audience, to the point where the term alternative no longer means anything. Alternative music is purely and simply the music kids are listening to today.

You want proof? *Out of Time* is one example. The even more astounding rise to preeminence of the Seattle punk rock band Nirvana in late 1991 and early 1992 is another. Witness, too, the surprise success that summer of the Lollapalooza tour, spearheaded by Jane's Addiction, and masterminded by that band's lead singer, Perry Farrell. That tour brought together seven disparate elements of the alternative rock community—Henry Rollins, Butthole Surfers, Ice-T, Nine Inch Nails, Siouxsie and the Banshees, Living Colour, and Jane's Addiction—on one bill, along with a potpourri of art, political and social issues, and, most importantly, strange food. These bands had been distinguished heretofore only by a common lack of mainstream acceptance (with the possible excep-

Above: "The secret of R.E.M.," says Michael Stipe, "is that Mike doesn't play bass like a bass player, Peter doesn't play guitar like a guitar player, and I don't sing like a singer. And Bill just sort of holds it all together."

Right: Irrespective of other developments in the music industry in 1991, it certainly was R.E.M.'s year.

tion of Living Colour). And yet this free-for-all attracted sell-out audiences everywhere it went, when even much-ballyhooed, long-awaited acts such as Guns N' Roses had trouble filling their bills.

All this meant that some sort of movement was slouching towards the suburbs and malls of America to be born. What had been merely a fringe of the record-buying public had by nearly imperceptible degrees become a significant slice, with the result that bands such as R.E.M., Nirvana, and Jane's Addiction achieved a measure of success that a few years back would have been unthinkable for bands as patently "left-field" as they are.

There's a negative side to the sea change taking place in American music, however—even as the mainstream expands to take in a good chunk of what was once the college rock fringe, true inno-

vation is being pushed farther and farther from the mainstream. The independent rock scene that nurtured R.E.M. and bands like them is slowly being crushed to death.

No, indie rock isn't dead, but it is, as Paul Westerberg of the Replacements recently said, going underground—the exact opposite of what happened with college rock. Five years ago the

thought of, say, Sonic Youth being on a major label would have been as unthinkable as it would have been undesirable; today, it would seem a gross injustice if they weren't. And hell, why not? These days, it seems as if the majors are buying up anything that moves, or at least moves noisily, as long as the band in question has some sort of independent credibility and/or following. This is good for the bands in the short run, and for some even in the long run, but the overall effect is hardly salutary, especially as it concerns the health of the independent system, which until now has developed and nurtured these bands.

Most likely, this mainstream bloat will deflate somewhat in the next couple of years as the majors realize that it's probably not a good idea to sign every half-assed jangly guitar rock band that comes their way. And that's gonna come as a shock to a lot of bands who signed up thinking they'd have a few years or at least a couple of albums to find their step. There'll be a whole bunch of unemployed clumsy rhythm-guitarist-poets in a couple of years—if you're planning on starting a band, you'll probably be able to pick one up real cheap.

Irrespective of other developments in the music industry in 1991, it certainly was R.E.M.'s year—tour or no tour. In retrospect, *Out of Time*'s success was almost inevitable and doesn't seem all that mysterious. It's a marvel of nonspecific pop. The album presents a potent distillation of everything R.E.M.'s ever been about: folkish instrumentation, ambiguous, Romantic lyrics, simple settings, and melodies. The whole is an affecting and subsequently much-copied blend, but R.E.M. manages to achieve that sound without really trying. Nothing the four of them play could ever not sound like R.E.M., and while "personality" is not first on my Virtues of Great Bands list, it sure as hell doesn't hurt.

Interestingly, *Out of Time*, for all its lush demeanor, was actually recorded in a remarkably straightforward manner. Many of the basic tracks were recorded live, with minimal overdubs, other than the vocals. "Low," according to Peter Buck, even used the scratch vocal track Stipe usually lays down as a guide while the band is recording basic rhythm tracks. The baroque quality of many of the songs stems both from the elegiac nature of

Above: Michael Stipe: "I don't really feel like I should be shackled to this image that every song I write has to be about the plight of the homeless."

Right: Out of Time, *for all its lush demeanor, was actually recorded in a fairly straightforward manner.*

much of the songwriting itself and from the instrumental flavors later added onto the spare basics. Buck attributes this lean style of recording to the amount of preproduction work the band habitually accomplishes before entering the studio, an R.E.M. tradition that stretches back to the *Chronic Town* days—although at that time "preproduction" consisted of playing the songs live a few hundred times. While the band has since lost that luxury, it has added considerable expertise in writing and arranging.

The first song on *Out of Time*, "Radio Song," is possibly the most experimental thing R.E.M.'s tried since the abortive pseudofunk of "Can't Get There From Here." Beginning with a typically pretty arpeggiated guitar intro and Michael portentously intoning "The world is collapsing around our ears / I turn on the radio," the song abruptly lurches into a leaden, Hammond organ-driven, Stax-type groove, over which Stipe bemoans both problems with a lover and an unfortunately appropriate song on the radio that, all unwanted, has clamped itself to the inside of his brain (these things, we all know, happen). "Radio Song" is saved from run-of-the-mill solipsism by the appositely cheery interjections of rapper KRS-One (from Boogie Down Productions), whose interest in what he calls the "edutainment" potential of pop—and especially rap—music had previously attracted the attention of Michael. KRS—or Chris, as his mom calls him—rides the song out with a spirited antiradio rap, chiding the whole generation of AOR addicts who grew up "All their lives / Radio listeners!"

"Losing My Religion," the smash hit single and the Grammy-winning video, succeeded, paradoxically, by its lack of personality—in other words, not because nobody understood what Michael

Stipe was singing about, but because everybody thought they did. That wasn't Stipe in the spotlight, that was everyone who ever sang along to the song (including me). Which, I guess, is what all good pop songs try to do—achieve some sort of universality of emotion. But the austerity of "Losing My Religion"'s setting helped make the song more evocative than just about anything else on AOR in 1991.

The "Losing My Religion" video cleaned up at the MTV awards, too. The video was the first where Stipe actually claimed authorship of the song by staring into the camera and lip-synching. Its simple, graceful, homoerotic imagery proved both affecting and relentlessly interesting—so that combined with the music, the video was nearly irresistible. The band consequently won seven well-deserved MTV awards, including Best Video (presaging its later Grammy). Stipe proved his usual eccentric self by showing up dressed in several layers of slogan-bearing T-shirts. (Of course, he stole that layers-o'-T-shirts thing from a woman named Mimi Goese of Hugo Largo, a band that Michael once produced. But Hugo Largo broke up a while back, so I guess it's okay.) It's interesting that after nearly ten years of solid touring-recording-touring, the one album R.E.M. decides not to tour behind goes ballistic, spawning heavy-rotation videos for "Losing My Religion" and "Shiny Happy People." Does this mean that big rock bands no longer need to tour if they make good videos?

Moving from "Radio Song" to "Losing My Religion" was less of a stylistic jolt before the latter became a megahit; it served at the time as what noted cultural critic Wayne Campbell would call a "palate cleanser," before slipping into the spare morbidity of "Low." "Low" was actually an older song that the band had played live more than a few times—the *Out of Time* version, greatly enhanced by Mike Mills's funereal organ accompaniment, legendary New Orleans horn player Kidd Jordan's haunting bass clarinet, and Bill Berry's stately, subdued percussion, is as raw and unaffected as anything the band's ever committed to polyethylene (or whatever CDs are made of).

"Near Wild Heaven," with its double lead vocal (Michael Stipe and Mike Mills) and borderline-

Right: Peter Buck: "I hate to sound like The Band in The Last Waltz, *but we basically spent the last ten years on the road. It [was] time to get away from it."*

Overleaf: On a strictly musical basis, Out of Time *is easily the most cohesive work the band had done sine Chronic Town.*

wimpy pop structure helps bridge the emotional chasm between the somber "Low" and "Endgame," whose Sam Beckett–derived title proves an apt description of its melancholic, wordless contents.

The following progression is an entirely natural one to the pure pop of "Shiny Happy People," whose message of unadulterated optimism Stipe insists is meant to be taken straightforwardly—even if it does sound like a bunch of people who've just taken a bunch of Ecstasy. The video for the song, featuring a group of shiny happy people (with the exception of Peter Buck, who looks pretty miserable), most of them friends of the band, cavorting in front of a mural painted by local schoolchildren, elicited strong reactions from some people. Lars Ulrich, drummer for speed metalers Metallica, said the video made him want to do "a John Bonham" with his television set. "Very unheterosexual," huffed the hairy rocker. The song is buttressed by vocals from Kate Pierson of the B-52's, marking the first appearance of female vocals on an R.E.M. track.

The tricky waltz-time intro to "Shiny Happy People" gave the band fits when laying down the basic tracks, according to Bill Berry. "We tried over and over to get the parts to fit together right, and in the end I still don't think we nailed it exactly," he says.

The spoken-word vocals to "Belong," the next song, were actually recorded on a Walkman by Michael in his garage. The enigmatic poetry of "Belong" was matched against a trademark Stipean, wordless, moaning chorus that lifted the song out of its art mire. "Half a World Away," which follows, continues the overall melancholic cast of the album, and contributes one of the most plangent melodies on the record.

"Texarkana" again features lead vocals from Mike Mills, and with its overlush string arrangement sounds, unfortunately, an awful lot like a Moody Blues song, an observation which will not be met with glee by any of the band members responsible. Nevertheless its lovelorn lyrics mesh nicely with the sappy arrangement, and the whole thing is just corny enough to come off likably. Besides, were the Moody Blues really so bad? (Yes.)

Which brings us to "Country Feedback," an almost instantaneous song both in the writing and in the recording, according to Peter Buck. Its curious use of feedback calls to mind some of the quieter Velvet Underground songs and counterbalances the prosaic song title. The lyrics are perhaps the bitterest—and certainly most personal sounding—on the record, combining the sense of regret and loss that occupies much of these songs with some of the vitriol of *Document*'s "The One I Love." "Me in Honey" is possibly the album's most determinedly rocking number. (There are few songs on *Out of Time* that actually rock. The result is that the album seems relentlessly fragile—I mean that in a good way—bordering on precious. I mean that in a good way, too.) Kate Pierson once again lends her pipes, and the insistent riff upon which the song is built propels the album to an uncharacteristically upbeat conclusion.

The past rumors of Michael Stipe's and Peter Buck's differences, especially around the time of *Life's Rich Pageant,* seemed completely laid to rest by the release of *Out of Time.* On a strictly musical level, the record is easily the most cohesive (both thematically in terms of lyrics and music, and in the care with which the songs were sequenced) work the band had done since *Chronic Town,* and that record was cohesive only because of the limited stylistic palette R.E.M. then possessed.

Certainly in interviews such as the following, conducted around the time of the release of *Out of Time,* the world views of the two leaders (despite all the efforts of the band to present themselves as a democracy, the public continues to view Buck and Stipe as co-bandleaders, which is partly the media's fault and partly a product of the fact that, um, it's partly true) have become so close as to become nearly indistinguishable. Undoubtedly

Right: Out of Time *had an elegiac, almost baroque quality to it, enhanced by the judicious use of unusual, non-R.E.M.–like instruments.*

this perception is to some degree aided by the improvement in the band's overall media savvy. Stipe, especially, has become notably adept at projecting a certain character not only on- but off-stage, which serves him in good stead during interviews. But it shows, above all, that the members of the band have settled into their separate roles more comfortably than most bands' members ever manage. More than anything else, the members of R.E.M. are in sync.

Why'd you call the album Out of Time?
Michael Stipe: Out of sheer desperation. We had all kinds of great names for it, but none that were applicable to the entire record. I mean, there's not one song that's a centerpiece, like "World Leader Pretend." We could've named *Green* that and said, well, that's what the album's about in a much broader way, but...I think that's kind of a cop-out. I think people should be able to come up with titles for things that are applicable to the entire thing. When we were fishing around for names, we were talking to all the people who worked at Paisley Park (Prince's studios, in Minneapolis, where the album was mixed) and there was this one secretary in particular that everyone was kind of endeared to, because she dressed really well. I think Mike was talking to her, and he said, you know, "the record's about memory and time and love," and she said, "How about something like 'in time?'" and he said "out of time" and that was it. Kind of a dull story, but that's what the record is about.

Out of Time—*like the Rolling Stones song?*
Stipe: Do they have a song called that? Well, fuck 'em. I think there's lots of meanings to it—you know, now that we're aging dinosaurs. We talked as a joke about doing our next photo session sitting in a public park around a chess board. We could wear those little hats and funny shoes.

Why are there no politics on the record this time? Or are there?
Stipe: No, there aren't really any politics on *Out of Time* at all. Every song on the record is a love song. And that's something I've never done before. Of course, I've written love songs, but they were pretty well obscure and oblique. These songs are about every kind of love—except maybe love of country. It's kind of, like—how can I say it without sounding like the leader of a movement? I guess I might be reacting to myself and thinking that I don't really feel like I should be shackled to this image that every song I write has to be about the plight of the homeless, concern for the environment, or

politics in general. I think there's only so far you can go writing songs like that and getting away with it. There are people who I think do it really well—Peter Garrett from Midnight Oil and Natalie Merchant from 10,000 Maniacs, I think, are brilliant at doing that kind of thing. I don't think I can do it all the time and I don't want to paint myself into a corner—into being a political folk singer with a rock band.

How far do you think you can take that without starting to sound preachy?
Stipe: I would think as far as I wanted to, because people are starved for information on anything political.

As simply as possible, what are the major differences between Out of Time *and, say,* Green, *or any of your previous records?*
Stipe: Well, just on a real simplistic level, there's instruments we use that we haven't explored before, or if we have it was in a real kind of textbook way. And now we're expanding with string sections and horn players and bringing people in from outside to do vocals, KRS-One and Kate Pierson from the B-52's. We brought in composers to work on string arrangements. We brought this great guy up from New Orleans, Kidd Jordan, who's a legendary blues horn player. There's one song he put on I guess five different horns.

Peter, there're a lot of guest musicians on this record.
Peter Buck: I like the idea that we can bring other people in. I was really surprised when Michael brought in other singers. Kate Pierson's got a great voice. And I think the KRS-One rap thing turned out great, too.

Do you like rap?
Buck: Yeah, but it's like everything else. Ninety-five percent of it's shit and the other five percent of it is great. Rap is funny because you hear all of these musicians saying, "Man, that's not playin', that's just rappin'." That's what they used to say about me. "He can't really play~!" you know? But it's not scales that make a good record. It's your ability to utilize your instrument, whether it's a guitar or a sampler.

Peter Holsapple [formerly of the dBs] plays guitar on most of the new songs. Are you comfortable recording

Right: Michael Stipe: "Every song on Out of Time *is a love song. And that's something I've never done before."*

with other guitarists?

Buck: It helps me knowing there's someone who'll play the riffs along with me so I can play something else. My goal is to record my parts strictly live and never do any overdubs. We apportioned the parts so that on six of the seven songs Peter Holsapple's on, I play the live instrument, the mandolin for example, right into a microphone. I'd like to do the next record totally live with side musicians. I like the idea of a performance.

Why didn't you tour for Out of Time*?*

Buck: I hate to sound like the Band in *The Last Waltz,* but we basically spent the last ten years on the road. It's time to get away from it. As much as I love touring, it's a big deal. We start planning six months ahead of time, hiring people, and spending a quarter of a million dollars building a stage. It's kind of like being in the army.

But you can't just show up at the Omni (an Atlanta arena) and decide to play there. One of the good things is that you get a lot of energy out of it, it's exciting to be caught up in it, going around the world with your friends.

Seems like it would be hard to play a lot of the Out of Time *stuff live.*

Buck: We could do it. Almost everything we've ever written, we can actually sit down and play together. It's just that a lot of things you've come to hear in the songs wouldn't be there: the string section, things like that. But given the three of us playing, and Michael singing, we can do most of the stuff very well. On some of the stuff you wouldn't even notice the strings weren't there.

You guys are awful prolific. I thought the plan was to

take six months off after Green *before you began writing songs for* Out of Time*, but weren't you back writing together within weeks of that tour's end?*

Buck: Well, what happened is that we did that tour and we knew that it was gonna kind of wear us out. We were at the point where ten months on the road wasn't necessarily what...it was what we should've done, but it was the kind of thing where we hadn't done it like that in a while. We were sure that we would be absolutely ill of each other's presence. And I remember Bill's Christmas party in 1989. We finished November 26 or something. He had his party on, like, the 18th or 19th of December and we all kind of were saying, like, maybe we should practice. So we started practicing January 2. We were supposed to have six months off. We turned out a bunch of stuff then that ended up on *Out of Time.*

Does it help that you have three different people, each writing music?

Buck: Sure, Bill or Mike will always be, like, "Well, I've got this thing." I mean, that's what we do. It's not some major creative thing. It's just something we do. If you do it long enough, you can do it without thinking about it. Once you get to the point where you realize that a million people or more are gonna listen to the record, you start getting a little tense. Your start thinking . . . but you know, I think your first creative impulses are always the best. The thing to try to do is get

Above, and facing page: Michael Stipe: "I think there's lots of meanings to Out of Time *— you know, now that we're aging dinosaurs. We talked as a joke about doing our next photo session in a public park around a chess board."*

to the point where you're good enough at it that you can do it without thinking about it. Of course, you go back and edit yourself a little bit and tighten things up. It's really nice. You write a song in one minute and record it in the next one.

We've kind of gotten back to doing that. A lot of stuff on the *Out of Time* record were the demos. "Country Feedback" is the demo. We didn't have a song. I walked in, I had four chords. I put them down with Bill playing bass. I put the feedback on it. John Keane put the pedal steel on it. Michael walked in and said, "Oh, I've got words for that." The next day he just sang it. The total recording time, not including the mix, was, like, 35 minutes. It's really nice if you can get it to flow like that.

Especially since a lot of that stuff on Out of Time *does sound like more effort than that went into it.*
Buck: That's mostly because we think it out beforehand. Most people that make records...almost every band that's successful, what they tend to do is they might write at home, but they don't rehearse. And then the week before the record they get together and bang some shit out and they put it down. With us, we just play stuff all the time—so that "Losing My Religion," we played that on and off in the studio for two months. When it first started out it was I think Bill on bass, Mike on organ and me on mandolin. We changed instruments a couple of times. At one point, I was playing it on guitar.

The idea of the record was to a use real spare kind of instrumentation but with strings and other stuff. Most of the tracks were cut live. Michael would redo his vocals. I think "Low" is the scratch vocal. "Losing My Religion," that's totally live, acoustic guitar, bass, mandolin, and drums. No overdubs, no changes. Mike put down the string part. And, in retrospect, I think it worked, obviously beyond our expectations in terms of popular success.

I guess it's difficult for a band to remove themselves in any appreciable way from the record they've just spent a considerable chunk of time and effort creating. This might account for the surprise with which the members of R.E.M. greeted *Out of Time*'s almost immediate success.

Some time in the spring of 1991, after the record had been out for about three weeks and was nearing the top of the charts, I ran into Bill Berry and Peter Buck in a hotel bar in Los Angeles. They were in the middle of a promo tour (press and radio only) for *Out of Time*, and I was in the middle of my second beer. Both of them expressed a degree of stupefaction at the runaway success of the record.

"It's amazing," quoth Bill. "I never expected this. I hoped it would do well, but..."

"Yeah, I remember," I replied. "You were afraid no one would get it. Well, I guess they got it."

"I guess they did," he said. "Can I buy you a beer?"

"Actually," I said, "could you buy me a car?"

"Don't push it, Jim."

So I didn't.

R.E.M.

C H A P T E R   5

B A C K   T O
T H E   F U T U R E
1 9 9 2 . . .

B
E
H
I
N
D
·
T
H
E
·
M
A
S
K

BACK TO THE FUTURE

I t's the week before the 1991 Grammy Awards, and the R.E.M. office on West Clayton is a hive of activity. Brook Johnson, R.E.M.'s office majordomo, is busy arranging transportation and hotels in New York City not only for the band but for their family members. It seems that everyone's family wants to go to the Grammys, resulting in a total of about 30 or 40 close friends and relatives descending on the city from different directions at the same time. "Yeah, I can tell my mom I'm on the cover of every Podunk magazine in the world," says Peter Buck, "but the Grammys are something she can grasp onto, something she can understand and tell her friends." One source of excitement for the family members

is the fact that they, as well as the band members, will have to register under assumed names (the lengths to which rabid fans will go to make contact with their idols is legendary). "Is it really like that?" Bill Berry's mom asks Brook, not realizing the compass of her son's fame.

Yes, it's really like that. In the year since the release of *Out of Time*, Mrs. Berry's son's band has become one of the most famous in the land, if not the world, on a par with Guns 'n' Roses or U2. It's not something anyone in the band would ever have dreamed possible, and at every new level of fame, the band has always expressed pessimism at its prospects for going any further. "We're not

going to win any Grammys," declares Buck confidently, despite that R.E.M. has been nominated for a mind-boggling seven. "Not that I care," he adds off-handedly, quickly reeling off his predictions for the winners in every category. His deter-

---

Above: Despite their facade of indifference, R.E.M. did care about the Grammys — if they didn't, they wouldn't have attended.

Right: Peter Buck: "The three of us — Bill, Mike, and I — usually rehearse by ourselves for about a month because Michael's running around doing videos and just running around."

mination to treat the awards ceremony with a certain degree of irreverence is later emphasized as he proudly points to his intended costume, laid out neatly on a couch in his house—a pair of green pajamas with matching bathrobe. "I've got someone to make me one of those sign-card things that flip over, like people use in cars, saying things like, 'Fantastic!' 'I'm overwhelmed!' 'Thanks, everyone!' " (This last idea apparently didn't pan out, as it was nowhere in evidence during the ceremony.)

But despite the facade of indifference, R.E.M. did care about the Grammys—if the band didn't it wouldn't have attended. And its excitement at winning the two awards it did—even if one of them was for best "alternative" band, a genre it belongs to about as much as Jethro Tull belonged to Heavy Metal when it won best band in that category a few years back—was apparent in the way Michael Stipe leapt to his feet when the award was announced. Even if he was eager just to make another political broadside, this time about the importance of voting for young people.

Everyone knows the Grammy ceremony is a great big enormous bore. The 1991 awards were no exception, especially considering that the lion's share went to Natalie Cole's exploitative snoozefest "Unforgettable." But the mere fact that R.E.M. was nominated for so many awards, in conjunction with the excitement caused by Nirvana's remarkable meteoric rise to stardom, pointed again to the sea change taking place in American music. That there was even a category

for so-called alternative rock meant, at least, that the mainstream had taken notice, much as it had a few years earlier with the institution of rap and heavy metal categories. The awards have never really pretended to be much more than a popularity contest, and even that popularity was limited to a fairly staid group of industry mavens, most of whom probably found Liza Minnelli a bit too cutting-edge for their tastes. So in that sense, R.E.M. certainly was an alternative rock act, although the fact that the band was nominated in the best pop group category, as well, didn't help to clarify matters any.

But if nothing else, the ceremony gave the band members another chance to rub elbows with genuine celebrities—and who can resist that?

"I met Quincy Jones once, at one of the awards ceremonies, awhile back," recalls Peter Buck of one of his more memorable celebrity encounters. "I was introduced to him. It was right when that Michael Jackson album—I think it was *Bad*—came out. Everyone was, like, in this receiving line. 'You should meet Quincy. We're gonna be on Warner Brothers.' So I said, 'Yeah, sure.' Everyone was telling him, 'Quincy, Quincy. *Bad*, great

Above: Despite their absorption in their own work after the release of Out of Time, *the individual members of R.E.M. were in this same period as busy as ever in projects outside of the band's normal purview.*

Right: Peter Buck: "When we sit and write songs, we don't sit there and go, 'We're giving them this gift of this genius inspiration.' No, we're shlubs that bang out some chords."

record.' I heard eight people say it. And I walked up and said, 'Man, those horn charts that you did for Ray Charles in the '50s were the best things I've ever heard.' And he went, 'All right!' That Ray Charles stuff changed my life. I mean, Michael Jackson's great, but it doesn't mean anything to me. I just wanted to tell Quincy that some of us younger folks do remember. Because Quincy was, like, 17, and he was doing horns with Ray. That incident in itself pretty much contains all the bad things and good things about awards ceremonies— at least, the things I think are bad and good. To be able to tell someone how much he meant to you. But to have to put up with the rest of the bullshit, or just even be involved with it in some way—I'm not sure it's worth it."

As frenetic as Grammy week may have been, it represented little more than a hiccup in the R.E.M. workaday routine. After all, the boys had another album to produce. Not touring behind *Out of Time*

(although the three-month promotional jaunt was in some ways similar to touring, with the exception that the band didn't actually have to go up onstage every night and play) left the group with an unusual amount of time on its hands, some of which it filled with side projects—producing bands (Michael Stipe and Peter Buck, of course, being the leaders in this field of activity) and making cameo appearances on friends' records and videos. (Peter Buck's house, along with Peter and Michael, made its MTV debut in a Billy Bragg video. "The director swore it wouldn't be recognizable as my house," says Peter, "but there it is, big as life.") The rest of the time was spent writing new songs—a process which hasn't grown any easier over time for the band, whose impressive productivity is more a result of its tireless work ethic than a limitless reservoir of inspiration.

"I wrote three songs in the last three days," says a grinning, self-satisfied Michael Stipe, in the midst

of preparing to leave Athens for the Grammy ceremony.

"So what's the new stuff like?" I ask. "Salsa metal? I heard it's the next big thing."

"Salsa metal? The next big thing?" ponders Michael. "Well, I guess it depends on who you ask. David Thomas [from Cleveland avant-garage band Pere Ubu] would probably tell you it's armies of accordions."

Whatever. The sound of the new record, whatever it eventually ends up being (and R.E.M. records, whatever their flaws, all tend to have a kind of cohesiveness of style, which is a very difficult and time-consuming thing to achieve), will doubtless be reached as the result of an evolutionary process—much the way the band itself has developed. There are very rarely any set-in-stone plans, just ideas that either do or don't sound cool and that either are or aren't executed to the satisfaction of the band members. It's a casual, almost laid-back, process that makes all the more impressive the number of quality songs the group manages to knock out, year in and year out.

Is it more difficult to write songs now that you're, um, more mature?

Peter Buck: Yeah, sure. When you're younger, you just tend to write more. You drop your pen, and that's a reason to write a song. It was easier then. Especially when you hadn't discovered how to write songs. An F chord for me was like a novelty. You'd write something in F, and you'd go, 'Wow, that's cool.' Whereas now, the inspiration—it's not harder, we write songs in a day or whatever. But in those days, it was like you were inventing it. So you didn't really know anything about songwriting.

Above: The sound of the next record, whatever it eventually ends up being, will doubtless be reached as the result of an evolutionary process — much the way the band itself has developed.

Right: Peter Buck: "We practice four or five days a week. I enjoy it. Athens is such a small town, I can bike down to the rehearsal hall."

Does having learned a certain amount of craft make it harder? I mean, do you now go, "No, you can't do that in a pop song," or whatever?

Buck: Yeah, you tend to. And also, you think, I've done that in the past. Now you also know what clichés are. In those days, you'd write it in A and it would have the I, IV, and V chords. It was like you invented it. I consciously try to get away from some of our writing styles. I don't know if people that listen can tell, but there was a whole year where everyone of our bridges only had two chords in it. It would go minor, major, minor, major, and then back to the major. You know. And then you realize, Gosh, we've been doing that minor-major thing at the bridge for a long time. Let's try to get a different kind of bridge.

Does part of your productivity stem from the fact that you guys seem to just like to play so damn much?

Buck: I guess so. We practice four or five days a week. I enjoy it. Athens is such a small town, I can bike down to the rehearsal hall. I don't know. We're just always writing songs. I don't really know why, other than—again, it's just what we do. If I were a furniture builder or something, you'd probably ask why I made so many end tables.

We were doing demos at John Keane's this week. We had about 24 or 25 we worked on, some of them we thought that sucked and some were good. And we ended up recording 18. We did like five more this week just 'cause we were in there, and Bill would go, 'Well, I've got another one.' So he'd put down bass and guitar and drum machine. Then I'd go in and put down acoustic guitar and have Mike put down the bass and Bill would put a drum to it. We came up with a whole lot of really cool stuff that way. It's all part of that thing, where if you do it long enough, you can do it without thinking. I think Michael, at this point, is trying to get things to flow a little bit easier, too. So he's kind of writing off the top of his head again.

Above: Peter Buck: "It's funny, 'cause the [Athens] city council, and all these people, are kind of admitting that most of the tourism of this town comes because of us."

Right: Jefferson, I think we're lost. Publicity photo for Out of Time.

Overleaf: As frenetic as Grammy week may have been, it represented little more than a hiccup in the R.E.M. workaday routine.

Is there any different idea with the new stuff, something that you did on Out of Time *that you do or don't want to do differently on this record? I remember last time we talked, you were saying, "With the next one we just want to be more basic, kind of stripped-down."*

Buck: I don't know. You always start out with an ideal about what you want to do, but it never— 'cause you just write songs whatever way inspiration strikes. One of the goals that we originally had with this was that we were gonna do all of this stuff, learn it, and then record it live. We'll have like ten players with us. We'll have a folk-rock-orchestra album. Whatever. If we're gonna have a string section, play it with us. And the stuff is all turning out different, so I don't know. We've got a bunch of weird kind of Arabic funk songs. We're kind of into this thing where we do a lot of modal feedback-y things. And with this kind of weird backbeat thing that Bill does, it's not actually funk. It's kind of like, if you were an Arab, you might

think it's funky. So I don't know how that stuff's going. We've got some stuff that sounds like us. We've got so many songs. It depends on which ones we finish.

Where are you recording?

Buck: I think Bearsville [in upstate New York] again, for the basic tracks. And then after that, it's up in the air.

Is Scott Litt coproducing again?

Buck: Yeah, he was in town this whole week, while we did demos. I think we ended up with 23 or 24 things that have been given pretty serious consideration. We threw out about four or five.

Can anyone just veto a song, knock it out of the running?

Buck: What happens is that the three of us—Bill, Mike, and I—rehearse by ourselves for about a month because Michael's running around. He's

doing videos and just running around. And since he doesn't play any instruments, if he sits there when we're working songs out, it can almost be deleterious to have him there because he doesn't play anything. He's like, "Oh, that's real great. Now speed it up twice as fast, throw away the chorus, write a new bridge, and change the key." "But Michael, that's a different song." We like to present him with finished ideas. We'll demo them, then he'll come in and do his thing.

That seems like a real sensible way to do things.
Buck: At this point, really, we've got about 24 on tape and it's really the ones that move him to finish them that will end up on the album. And one of the things we've learned is that the earlier it is on the tape, the more likely he is to finish it. So we stick our favorites at the beginning. Even on *Out of Time*, we put our three least favorite songs first because we figured we were getting them out of the way. And he just loved them and finished them. But it turned out really good. One of them is the one on that Wim Wenders soundtrack, that *Until the End of the World* movie thing. We hate that song. We wrote it and put it down and he just sings it—the first song on the tape. And we're like, 'Michael, that was the worst song we

wrote this whole year.' It's, like, first on the tape.

Despite their absorption in their own work, the individual members of R.E.M., who have always found time to indulge in extracurricular activities, were in this same period as busy as ever in projects outside of the band's normal purview. Stipe, as ever, the extramusical dabbler, continued to experiment in video and film (his influence over the band's "Losing My Religion" video changed R.E.M.'s minds somewhat about video's inherent evils), and took the time as well to pen articles on responsible consumerism and environmentalism for *Spin* and *Sassy* magazines ("I don't drink tap water; chlorine makes me retch") and take part in a number of politically-oriented forums ("Now I can hold a press conference on toxic waste," Stipe has said, "and it doesn't have to go into the songs"). In addition to the nonmusic activity, he's

---

Above: Peter Buck: "I think Michael at this point is trying to get things to flow a little bit easier. He's kind of writing off the top of his head again." Stipe with Arsenio Hall at the MTV Awards.

Right: In addition to the non-music activity, Stipe's also taken the time to support Earth Day events.

also taken the time to produce a slew of Athens bands, four of which he presented at a special showcase during the annual New Music Seminar in New York in July 1991.

Mike Mills and Bill Berry kept somewhat quieter—perhaps unnerved by their Hindu Love Gods experience. Besides, Berry, for one, says, "When R.E.M.'s over, I'll do more producing and stuff. I'm probably lazier in that way than the other guys. Life's too short. When I'm off, I'm off. I play golf, ski, go to my lake house. When I'm 40, bald, and getting a little rounder, I'll think about those things."

Peter Buck, as noted earlier, can't seem to keep his hands off of his guitar and, as a result, plays on or produces close to three-fourths of all the records issued in any given year (this is, possibly, an exaggeration). Despite the fact that an inordinate number of the bands currently resident in Athens weren't from there originally, and that a lot of them move there in hopes of being seen and, consequently, produced by a member of R.E.M. ("It happens," Buck admits), Peter never seems to be able to resist.

"You've got to understand," explains the guitarist, "that most people that move here come from small towns. Like, no one moves here from Los Angeles. No one moves here from New York. It's always Gainesville, Florida, or Bumfuck, Alabama. There's nothing going on in those towns. You're not gonna move to New York. You're not gonna move to L.A. You drown out there. You fuckin' drown. You have to pay to play. You have to pay to rehearse. Here, you can move to town and for a hundred bucks find a place to rehearse. You can play. I know people who play twice a month and live off it. Not well, but—it's a cheap town and there are a lot of things going on here.

"People do come through here. People from record companies. I just did the Dashboard Saviors' record. They're a local band, and they weren't even really drawing well locally, although they're a cool band. I brought a friend of mine from Twin Tone to see them, and he liked them and signed them. And they were kind of like, 'Wow.' They moved here from West Virginia to come to Athens. I was talking to one of their band members. He goes, 'Man, all the guys from West Virginia, we're heroes to them. We moved to Athens, got a record deal and got produced by Peter Buck.' "

Besides his production activity, Buck seems ever willing to lend a riff or two to whoever comes through town, which leads to some unlikely combinations.

I heard that you just did a cover of [seminal British folkie] Nick Drake's "Pink Moon" with the Psychedelic Furs' Richard Butler.
Buck: Yeah, it sounds really good. I met Richard—we'd bumped into each other on and off for years. I think earlier in both our lives, we would be drinking a little more and being bad boys. And so we're all a little bit older and more or less sober now. He's totally sober, right, and "I don't really drink much anymore," you know, he says, as he quaffs a beer. He came over my house when they were in town, and we were playing records and stuff. And he said, 'Do you know much about Nick Drake?' And I said I'm a huge Nick Drake fan. And he says, 'Well, I've been asked to do this compilation thing. What song should I do?' Well, I've always thought "Pink Moon" is kind of like an English version of [Robert Johnson's] "Hell Hound on My Trail."

It is really incredibly scary.
Buck: And I was talking to one of the guys from the band and he goes, "Well, why do you think it's a scary song?" The words, man: "Pink moon gonna get you all." It's just like—"Pink Moon," that's the end. It's death. It's about death, isn't it? He was like, "Well, if that's the way you want to read it." Our version's got a lot of feedback and then cellos and then swoopy pedal steel stuff. It sounds great. I think it's really wonderful.

Visiting Athens these days is not an entirely different experience from visiting the place, say, in 1980, as far as outward appearances are concerned. The place remains, first and foremost, a college town, with all that the term connotes: lots of beer-drinking, football-crazed frat idiots, sporadic bursts of culture, and a handful of snot-nosed intellectual brats running around on LSD, re-inventing bohemia. As far as the actual buildings are concerned, although Tyrone's burned down long ago (it's a parking lot today) and the church on Oconee Street no longer exists, you can still, if you want, trace the whereabouts of all six or seven incarnations of the 40 Watt Club—for instance, right down to its current spacious quarters. Even now, the place is quartered mere blocks from its original incarnation in Curtis Crowe's loft.

So you could easily be fooled into thinking things are pretty much as they were then. After all, the members of R.E.M. all still live here (to their occasional chagrin, when doe-eyed fans root through Michael Stipe's garbage or steal things off Peter Buck's porch or crash a band member's private party). There're still a lot of bands here. Rent's still cheap. (A friend once opined that the proliferation of Athens bands never should have been cause for wonder: "Cheap rent, places to play, and a continuously refreshed supply of freshmen girls—who wouldn't start a band?") So, apart from the star seekers, no real difference, right?

Well, not quite. There's a certain subtle, but all-important—at least in the eyes of the people who were around at the time—difference. There's no fun anymore. Go to a typical college rock-type show at the 40 Watt, and you'll see a crowd of clean-cut young kids, for the most part, just somberly standing around and politely clapping at the end of each song—no matter who the artist is. Back in the days, everyone was dancing, everyone was screaming, everyone was having a blast. Now that the stakes are so much higher, now that everyone who plays in town seems to have "making it" as their priority rather than "having a good time," a lot of the original magic is gone (at least, if you ask those who were there in the early days).

And in a way, albeit an indirect way, that's R.E.M.'s fault. Which probably helps explain why the band is so eager to put back into the town what the town so generously gave it.

It must be kind of weird to be almost like a tourist attraction in a way or a career enhancer when all you

---

Above: Things certainly turned out differently for R.E.M. than the band ever expected lo those many years ago, plugging in its amps on the rotting floorboards of the church on Oconee Street.

Right: Stipe, as ever the extra-musical dabbler, continues to experiment in video and film.

want to do is come home and do your job and hang out.
Buck: We think of it in a really non-Romantic way. The most Romantic that I ever think about is I manage to make my living using my mind. I'm proud of that. Really, when we sit and write songs, we don't sit there and go, This is a slice of someone's life. We're giving them this gift of this genius inspiration. No, we're shlubs that bang out some chords. Other people tend to take it real seriously. We take it seriously as far as doing it right, but on the other hand, we'll write some song and Mike will go, "Oh man, that's a deathless piece of shit." You know, you just write songs.

It's funny 'cause the city council, and all these people, are kind of admitting that most of the tourism of this town now comes from people coming because of us, because of the rock'n'roll scene. And they're trying to figure out a way to promote it without giving away our phone numbers. They said, Well, we want to have some kind of thing here, but we can't tell them where the people in R.E.M. live.

Yeah, like put a sign out front. "Home of Peter Buck of R.E.M."
Buck: We were actually part of a tour for a while. Buses would come by and stuff—not because of who we were but because we're on this trail of old homes. But then somebody at the local tourist office started saying, like, "In this old-home section, this is where Peter Buck and this is where Bill Berry lives." We'd have people come to the house and go, "They told us at the visitors' center where you lived." We had to call them and sort of, um, request that they stop doing that.

I was going through some posters from the very early days of the Athens scene last night and there was a poster from a party at this address.
Buck: Yeah, this used to be a crazy house. That's one reason why I bought it—I've always loved this house. I used to come to parties here. It was the kind of place—they had a big swing on that tree. So everyone would be swinging and you'd walk in the door and there'd be someone naked, passed out, face-first. There was a ten-foot-tall painting of Jimi Hendrix in the hallway. Eight apartments in here. Some of the guys from Love Tractor used to live here. Sam Seawright, who's a painter—I own a couple of his paintings. A lot of my friends lived in this place, so I'd been over here all the time. It was just this crazy, rocked-out, hippie, drug house. And so when they fixed it up, I said, "I've always liked that house. Well, I'm gonna buy it." I didn't even own a car. I owned two houses, and I didn't own a car.

I hope you had a bike to get back and forth.
Buck: That's the thing. My brother said, "You must be the only person in the history of the world that owns two houses and doesn't own a car." Who needs a car?

Well, I guess here, you really don't—everything seems to be around the corner from everything else.
Buck: I'm three-quarters of a mile from downtown. I can walk. It's great 'cause I like to have a drink now and again, and I don't drive and drink ever, 'cause it's wrong. So I tend to leave my car downtown, sometimes weeks at a time. I'll just leave it at the office 'cause it's right downtown. It's parked right at the office. Like if I have two glasses of wine, I'll just go, "I'm not gonna drive" and just leave it. I don't need the car for maybe four days. One day I'll look out and realize that I don't have a car in my driveway. The only time I use the car is when I go out to the mall to see a movie. I hate going to the mall, but they have a real big screen there. The mall sucks, though. I hate malls.

Yeah, things sure turned out much differently for R.E.M. than the band ever expected lo those many

Above: "I think we're still great," says Michael Stipe. "And I don't think I have blinders on. We've done pretty incredible things, and I'm proud of it."

years ago, plugging in its amps on the rotting floorboards of the church on Oconee Street. But despite the changes time hath wrought both on the band and on the town it loves, it doesn't seem as though the band members would want it any other way.

"I think we're still great," says Michael Stipe. "And I don't think I have blinders on. I had no desires or goals at the beginning. We never had any idea of what was possible. We've done pretty incredible things, and I'm proud of it. I spent a great deal of time doing it.

"Would I do it all again, if I had the opportunity? I'm an unbelievably happy person now, so I'd say, 'Fuck yeah, I'd do it again.'

Fuck yeah, he'd do it again. That's pretty much the R.E.M. attitude, if such a thing exists, in a nutshell. Not even to "do it again," but just—at the risk of sounding like a sneaker commercial—to do it. So far, it's served the band well.

C H A P T E R 6

D I S C O G R A P H Y,
T O U R S, A N D
G U E S T A P P E A R A N C E S

R.E.M.

**B
E
H
I
N
D
·
T
H
E
·
M
A
S
K**

Commercially Issued 7" Singles

"Radio Free Europe" / "Sitting Still"
Hib-Tone HT-0001 US 7/81
"Wolves, Lower" (flexidisc)
Trouser Press #12 US 12/82
"Radio Free Europe" (LP version) / "There She Goes
Again"
IRS IR-9916 US 4/83
"Radio Free Europe" (edited) / "There She Goes Again"
IRS IR-9916 US 4/83
"Radio Free Europe" / "There She Goes Again"
IRS PFP 1017 UK 8/83
Illegal NL 8/83
"So. Central Rain (I'm Sorry)" / "King of the Road"
IRS IR-9927 US 5/84
IRS IRS 105 UK 3/84
Illegal ES971 Aust 84
IRS A 4255 NL 6/84
IRS IR 9927 CAN 84
"(Don't Go Back to) Rockville" / "Wolves, Lower"
IRS IRS107 UK 6/84
IRS ILSA 3567 NL 84
IRS Illegal SP 84
"(Don't Go Back to) Rockville" (edited version, 3:51) /
"Catapult" (live)
IRS IR-9931 US 8/84
"Tighten Up" (flexidisc)
"Bucketfull of Brains" UK 3/85
"Can't Get There From Here" / "Bandwagon"
IRS IRS 52642 USA 6/85
IRS IRM102 UK 7/85
Illegal SP 85
IRS 6384 NL 85
"Driver 8" / "Crazy"
IRS IRS52678 USA 6/85
"Can't Get There From Here" / "Driver 8"
IRS ES 1082 Aust 85
"Wendell Gee" / "Crazy"
IRS IRM.105 UK 9/85
IRS ILSA6587 NL 9/85
"Wendell Gee" / "Crazy" / "Ages of You" / "Burning
Down"
IRS A6587 NL 9/85
"Femme Fatale" (flexidisc)
The Bob US 6/86
"Fall on Me" / "Rotate Ten"
IRS IRS52883 US 7/86
IRS IRM 121 UK 9/86
IRS ILSA 7302 NL 9/86
IRS ES 1170 NL 86
IRS 52883 CAN 86
"Superman" / "White Tornado" IRS
IRS 52971 US 11/86
IRS IRM 128 UK 86
IRS 650225 7 AUST 86
IRS ILS 650225 7 NL 86
IRS 52971 CAN 86
"The One I Love" / "Maps and Legends" (live)
IRS IRS 53171 US 9/87

IRS 53171 NL 88
"Finest Worksong" (LP version) / "Time After Time"
IRS ILS 651320 7 NL 88
"It's the End of the World as We Know It (And I Feel
Fine)" / "This One Goes Out" (live)
IRS IRM651348 7 AUST 87
"It's the End of the World as We Know It"
IRS 53220 CAN 88
"It's the End of the World as We Know It" / "Last
Date"
IRS IRS651348 7 AUST 87
"The One I Love" / "Last Date"
IRS IRM 146 UK 11/87
"The One I Love" / "Maps and Legends" (live)
IRS ILS6511137 NL 87
"It's the End of the World As We Know It (And I Feel
Fine)"(1-sided)
IRS ARI2066 SP 87
"Finest Worksong" / "Time After Time," etc.
IRS ILS651320.7 NL 88
"Orange Crush" / same
Warner Bros. PRO-523 GERM 88
Warner Bros. 1.008 SP 88
"Pop Song '89" / "Orange Crush"
Warner Bros. PRO-541 GERM 88
"Parade of the Wooden Soldiers" / "See No Evil"
R.E.M. Fan Club US 12/88
"Pop Song '89"/ same
Warner Bros. PRO-76407 Can 89
"Stand" / same
Warner Bros. 7.27688 US 89
Warner Bros. 1.033 SP 89
"Turn You Inside Out" / same
Warner Bros. 1.087 SP 89
"Academy Fight Song" / "Good King Wenceslas"
R.E.M. Fan Club US 12/89
"Get Up" / same
Warner Bros. 7.22791 US 89
"Shiny Happy People"
Warner Bros. 1378 SP 91

Commercially Issued 12" Singles and EPs

"Talk About Passion" / "Shaking Through" / "Carnival
of Sorts (Boxcars)" / "1,000,000"
IRS PFSX 1026 UK 11/83
"So. Central Rain (I'm Sorry)" / "Voice of Harold" /
"Pale Blue Eyes"
IRS IRSX 105 UK 3/84
IRS A12.4255 NL 3/84
"(Don't Go Back to) Rockville" / "Wolves" / "9-9"
(live) / "Gardening at Night" (live)
IRS IRSX107 UK 6/84
IRS A12.4734 NL 6/84
Illegal A12.4734 SP 84
"Can't Get There from Here" (extended mix) /
"Bandwagon" / "Burning Hell"
IRS IRT102 UK 7/85
IRS ILSA12-6384 NL 85

"Wendell Gee" / "Crazy" / "Driver 8" (live)
  IRS IRT105 UK 10/85
"Wendell Gee" / "Driver 8" (live)/ "Ages of You" /
  "Burning Down"
  IRS A12.587 NL 9/85
"Fall on Me" / "Rotary Ten" / "Toys in the Attic"
  IRS IRMT 121 UK 7/86
"Superman" / "White Tornado" / "Femme Fatale"
  IRS IRMT 128 UK 86
"Superman" / "White Tornado" / "Perfect Circle"
  IRS ILS6502556 NL 4/86
"It's the End of the World As We Know It (And I Feel
  Fine)" / "This One Goes Out" (live) / "Maps and
  Legends" (live)
  IRS IRMT 145 UK 8/87
"The One I Love" / "Last Date" (live) / "Disturbance at
  the Heron House"
  IRS IRMT146 UK 11/87
"The One I Love" / "The One I Love" (live) / "Maps
  and Legends" (live)
  IRS IRS23792 US 8/87
"The One I Love" / "Last Date" (live)/ "Disturbance at
  the Heron House"
  IRS ILS 6511136 NL 87
"Finest Worksong" (lengthy club mix) / "Finest
  Worksong" (other mix) / "Time After Time"
  IRS ILS6513206 NL 88
"Finest Worksong" (club mix) / "Finest Worksong"
  (other mix) / "Time After Time" (live)
  IRS IRS23850 US 3/88
  IRS IRMT 161 UK 4/88
"The One I Love" / "Fall on Me" / "So. Central Rain
  (I'm Sorry)"
  IRS IRMT173 UK 10/88
"Stand" / "Memphis Train Blues" / "(The Eleventh
  Untitled Song)"
  Warner Bros. W7577T UK 1/89
"Orange Crush" / "Ghost Rider" / "Dark Globe"
  Warner Bros. W2690T UK 5/89
"Stand" / "Pop Song '89" (acoustic version) /
  "Skintight" (live)
  Warner Bros. W2833T UK 8/89
"Losing My Religion" / "Rotary 11" / "After Hours" /
  Warner Bros. W0015T UK 91
"Shiny Happy People" / "Forty Second Song" / "Losing
  My Religion" (live acoustic)
  Warner Bros. WOO27T UK 91
"Near Wild Heaven" / "Pop Song '89" (live) / "Half a
  World Away" (live, Rockline)
  Warner Bros. W0055T UK 8/91

Promotional and Other
Non-Commercial 12" Singles and EPs

"Talk About the Passion" / "Catapult" / "Sitting Still"
  IRS SP70968 US 83
"Pretty Persuasion" / "(Don't Go Back to) Rockville"
  (edited 3.54)
  IRS SP70979 US 84
"(Don't Go Back to) Rockville" (edited 3.54) /

"Catapult" (live)
  IRS SP70982 US 84
"Can't Get There From Here" (radio edit 3.09) /
  "Driver 8" / " Life and How to Live It"
  IRS L33-17004 US 85
"Driver 8" / "Driver 8" (live)
  IRS L3317034 US 85
"Fall on Me" / same
  IRS L3317159 US 85
"Life and How to Live It" / "Bandwagon" / "Crazy"
  IRS L33-17060 US 85
"Fall on Me" / " Rotary Ten" / " Toys in the Attic"
  IRS IRMT121di UK 9/86
"I Believe" / "Toys in the Attic"
  IRS L33-17199 US 86
"Superman" / same
  IRS L33-17200 US 11/86
"Ages of You" / same
  IRS SP70416 US 87
"The One I Love" / same
  IRS L33-17384 US 87
"It's the End of the World as We Know It (And I Feel
  Fine)" / "Disturbances at the Heron House" (live)
  IRS L33-17430 US 87
"Finest Worksong" (media version) / "Finest
  Worksong" (untouched version)
  IRS L33-17510 US 88
"Orange Crush" / same
  Warner Bros. PRO-A-3306 US 88
"The One I Love"
  IRS WIRMT173ADL UK 87

Commercially Available Albums
and Mini-Albums

Chronic Town (mini LP)
  IRS SP70502 US 8/82
  IRS NL 84
Murmur
  IRS SP70014 US 4/83
  IRS SP70604 US 83
  IRS SP70604 UK 8/83
  Illegal ILP25433 NL 83
Murmur
  CBS/Sony 25AP-2659 JAP 83
Reckoning
  IRS IRSA7045 UK 4/84
  IRS ILP25915 SP 84
  IRS 28AP2847(IR) JAP 84
  IRS ILP25915 NL 84
  IRS CBS 25915 ISR 8?
Fables of the Reconstruction
  IRS IRS5592 US 6/85
  IRS MIRF1003 UK 6/85
  IRS IRS26525 NL/ SP 85
  IRS IRS26525 PORT 85
  IRS IRS28AP3058(IR) JAP 85
  Epic 144.877 BR 85
  Epic QEl25105 PH 8?
  IRS 26525 ISR 8?

Life's Rich Pageant
  IRS IRS5783 US 7/86
  IRS MIRG1014 UK 8/86
  Epic 144.905 BR 85
Dead Letter Office (compilation)
  IRS SP70054 US 4/87
  IRS SP70054 UK 5/87
  Epic 235.502 BR 87
  IRS ILP450961 GERM 87
Document
  IRS IRS42059 US 9/87
  IRS MIRG1025 UK 5/87
  IRS 28AP3382 JAP 87
  IRS ILP460105 NL/AUST87
untitled interview picture disc
  Baktabak Bak2057 UK 10/87
  Rapid Mouth Movement
  Pow Wow Pow 01 UK 88
Eponymous (compilation)
  IRS IR6262 USA 10/88
  IRS MIRG1038 UK 10/88
  IRS 4631471 GERM 88
Green
  Warner Bros. 25795 US 11/88
  Warner Bros. WX_234 UK 11/88
  Warner Bros. 670.8035 BR 11/88
  Warner Bros. 925795 GERM 11/88
  Warner Bros. 925795 SP 11/88
  Warner Bros. BAN925795 ISR 88
Out of Time
  Warner Bros. 7599-26496-1 UK 91
  Warner Bros. 7599-26496-1 GE RM 91

Radio Promotional Albums

Live Radio Concert (double LP)
  The Source, Concert, NBC 84-24 US 84
PFM Guest DJ Series
  GDJ84-133 Show#133 US 10/84
BBC Rock Hours
  London Wavelength BC603 US 1/85
In Concert
  BBC Transcription Services 04516 UK 5/85
R.E.M. '85
  Interview series #33 Show #13 US 85
In Concert (double LP)
  Westwood One Radio Networks IC86-24 US 11/86
Off the Road Special (double LP)
  Westwood One Radio Networks
  Show #89-09 US 2/89
Timothy White's Rock Stars (double LP)
  Westwood One Radio Networks
  WO 89-c US 3/89
The 1989 Isle of Dreams Festival
  Westwood One Radio Networks US 9/89
In Concert (triple LP)
  Westwood One Radio Networks IC-89 US 89
In Concert
  BBC Transcription Service CN4516/S
Stars of the Superstars (triple LP set)
  Westwood One Radio Networks CO8933 US 89

R.E.M. Tracks Included on Various Artist Compilation Albums, 12" EPs, and CDs

"Gardening at Night," *A New Optimism*
  Situation Two SITU 11 UK 12/84
"Windout" *Bachelor Party* (film soundtrack)
  IRS IRSAA 7051 UK
  IRS ILP 26138 NL
"Harbourcoat," *KROQ Presents the Normal Noise of IRS*
  IRS 28 AP 2830 (IR) Jap 84
"Radio Free Europe," *Just What the Doctor Ordered*
  IRS ILP 26807 NL 85
"Can't Get There From Here," *New Rock Collection*
  CBS 950.104 (promo only) Brazil/85
"Ages of You," *Live! For Life*
  IRS IRS 5731 US 5/86
  IRS MIRF 1013 UK 5/86
"(All I Have to Do Is) Dream"; "Swan Swan H,"
  Athens, GA—Inside Out (film soundtrack)
  IRS 6185 USA 87
"Fall on Me"; "(All I Have to Do Is) Dream,"
  The Best of IRS
  IRS LSP 980142 1 Greece 87
"Radio Free Europe"; "Fall on Me"
  Kickin' Back to the Future (CD)
  CBS/Sony32 DP 843 JAP/87
"The One I Love" *The IRS Singles*
  IRS MIRL 1501 UK 88
"Romance," *Made in Heaven* (film soundtrack)
  Elektra 9 60729 US 88
"Deck the Halls" *Winter Warnerland*
  (promo-only double LP compilation)
  Warner Bros. PRO A 3328(LP)
  PRO CD 3328(CD) USA 12/88
"Orange Crush," *Promo Disco International No. 62*
  (promo-only 12" EP)
  WEA 6WP 0065 BR 88
"Stand" *Promo Disco Internacional* (promo-only 12" EP)
  WEA Brazil
"Stand" *Rock Star Special 1*
  WEA 6WP.1008 BR
"It's the End of the World as We Know It,
  Greenpeace—Breakthrough
  Melodia A60 0043 008 RU 89
"It's the End of the World as We Know It,"
  Greenpeace—Rainbow Warriors
  RCA PL74065 EURO 6/89
"Turn You Inside Out," *Follow Our Tracks*
  (Promo-only compilation)
  Warner Bros. PRO-CD 3503(CD) US 89
"Superman," *These People Are Nuts* (compilation CD)
  IRS IRSD-82010 US 89
"Cool It" (30-second public service announcement for
  the National Wildlife Federation by Michael Stipe),
  CMJ Presents Certain Damage, Vol. 23 (2 CD set)
"I Walked With a Zombie"; "Where the Pyramid
Meets the Eye," *Tribute to Roky Erickson* (CD)
  Sire/Warner Bros. WA-2644-22 90

"Just What the Doctor Ordered"
   IRS ILP26807 ISR 85

Radio Promotional CDs

Up Close
Media American Radio 8908 US 3/89

Commercially Issued
Compact Disc Singles and EPS

"The One I Love" / "Last Date" / " Disturbance at the
   Heron House" (live)
   IRS DIRM 146 UK 11/87
"Finest Worksong" (other mix) / same (lengthy club
   mix) / "Time After Time, etc."   (note: 3" CD)
   IRS ILS651320 2 NL 4/88
"The One I Love" / "So. Central Rain (I'm Sorry)" /
   "Fall on Me"
   IRS DIRM173 UK 4/88
"Stand" / "Memphis Train Blues (Eleventh Untitled
   Song)"
   Warner Bros. W7577CD UK 1/89
"Stand" / "Memphis Train Blues"
   Warner Bros. 7599-27688-2 US 89
"Orange Crush" / "Ghost Riders" / "Dark Globe"
   Warner Bros. W2960 CD UK 5/89
"Stand" / "Pop Song '89" (acoustic) / "Skintight"(live)
   Warner Bros. W2833 CD UK 8/89
"Stand" / "Pop Song '89" (acoustic) / "Skintight"(live)
   Warner Bros. W2833CDX UK 8/89

Promotional & Other
Non-Commercial Compact Disc Singles

"It's the End of the World as We Know It (And I Feel
   Fine)" / "Finest Worksong" / " The One I Love"
   IRS DIRM146 UK 87
"It's the End of the World as We Know It (And I Feel
   Fine)" (edited version) / same (LP version)
   IRS CD45-17476 US 87
"Orange Crush"
   Warner Bros. PRO-CD 3306 US 88
"Stand"
   Warner Bros. PRO-CD 3353 US 1/89
"Pop Song '89"
   Warner Bros. PRO-CD 3357 US 5/89
"Turn You Inside Out"
   Warner Bros. PRO-CD 3446 US 89
"Get Up" (LP version) / "Orange Crush" (live) / "Turn
   You Inside Out" (live)
   Warner Bros. PRO-CD 3716 US 90

Commercially Issued
Compact Disc Albums

Murmur
   IRS AM70014 US 83

IRS CD70014 UK 89
Reckoning
   IRS AM70044 US 84
   IRS CD70044 UK 89
   IRS CDA7045 UK 85
Fables of the Reconstruction
   IRS MC5592 USA 85
   IRS DMIRF1003 UK 4/87
   IRS DMIRL1053 UK 87
Life's Rich Pageant
   IRS MC5783 US 7/86
   IRS DMIRG1014 UK 12/87
Dead Letter Office & Chronic Town
   IRS AM70054 US 4/87
   IRS CDA70054 UK 5/87
Document
   IRS MC42059 US 9/87
   IRS IRSD42059 UK 87
   IRS DMIRG1025 UK 10/87
Eponymous
   IRS MC6252 US 10/88
   IRS DMIRG1038 UK 11/88
Green
   Warner Bros. WA25795 US 11/88
   Warner Bros. 9257952 GERM 11/88
The Collection (5-CD set in slip box)
   IRS 46588.2 NL 8/90
   including:
   Fables of the Reconstruction (CDILP 26525)
   Life's Rich Pageant (CDILP 57064)
   Document (ILP 460105.2)
   Dead Letter Office (ILP 450961.2)
   Eponymous (ILP4631472)

Bootlegs

The Byrds Fly South
Uptown Lounge, Athens, GA (Roger McGuinn concert,
backed by R.E.M.)
1 LP: "Sunshine Love" / "The Tears "/ "Chestnut Mare"
"Tiffany Queen" / "You Ain't Going Nowhere" / "I'll
Feel a Whole Lot Better" / "Mr. Spaceman" / "The Bells
of Rhyme" / "Mr. Tambourine Man" / "Turn, Turn,
Turn" / "Eight Miles High" / "Knockin' on Heaven's
Door"

Can't Get There from Here
Hammersmith Palais Ballroom, London, England
10/28/85
2 LP: "Feeling Gravity's Pull" / "Harborcoat" / "Green
Grow the Rushes" / "Maps and Legends" / "Pilgrimage"
"Driver 8" / "Sitting Still" / "Good Advice" / "So.
Central Rain" / "Have You Ever Seen the Rain" / "Can't
Get There from Here" / "Seven Chinese Brothers" /
"Auctioneer" / "Old Man Kensey" / "Pretty Persuasion"
"Life and How to Live It" / "Second Guessing" /
"Rockville" / "Toys in the Attic" / "Radar Love" /
"Burning Hell" / "Talk About the Passion" / "Little
America"

Chronic Murmuring
1980–1981 early rehearsal; I.R.S. demos and *Chronic Town* rough mixes
2 LP: Garage Rehearsal, 1980: "Dangerous Times" / "I Don't Want You Anymore" / "Different Girl" / "Narrator" / "Just a Touch" / "Baby I" / "Mystery to M" "Permanent Vacation." I.R.S. Demos, 1981: "1,000,000" / "Ages of You" / "Gardening at High" / "Carnival of Sorts (Boxcars)" / "Stumble." *Chronic Town* Rough Mixes: "Catapult" / "Wolves, Lower" / "Laughing" / "Easy Come Easy Go" / "Shaking Through" / "Carnival of Sorts (Boxcars)" / "Stumble" / "Wolves, Lower" / "1,000,000" / "Windout" (sung by Jefferson Holt and Bert Downs) / "Just a Touch"

Do You Remember (Dead Giveaway Office)
Various Live, 1981–1986
Tyrone's, Athens, GA: "Welcome to the Starlight" / "Twentieth–Century Boy" / "Pills" / "Barney Miller Theme" / "Secret Agent Man" / "Hootnanny" / "DOA/Rave On." Golden Palominos, The Ritz, New York, 1/9/86; Omaha Peppermint Lounge, New York City 10/1/89: "So You Want to Be a Rock and Roll Star" / "Pale Blue Eyes" / "I Can't Control Myself" / "Femme Fatale." Unknown source: "I Got You Babe" / "Moon River" / "Crazy"

Documentary
Bren Events Center, Irvine, CA, 11/14/87
2 LP: "Finest Worksong" / "These Days" / "Welcome to the Occupation" / "Exhuming McCarthy" / "Don't Call on Me" / "Felling Gravity's Pull" / "King of Birds" / "I Believe" / "Maps and Legends" / "Driver 8" / "Superman" / "Auctioneer (Another Engine)" / "Oddfellows" / "Local 151" / "Earthquake Story" / "End of the World" / "Begin the Begin" / "Strange" / "Roller Show" / "Cuyahogs" / "Fall on Me" / "The One I Love" / "Crazy" / "Eat the Fucking Rich" (untitled) / "Just a Touch" / "After Hours"

Down South
Various Live 1981–1982
1 LP: Tyrone's, Athens, GA, 1/10/81: "Shaking Through" / "Rockville" / "Gardening at Night" / "Sitting Still" / "Burning Down" / "Get on the Way" / "There She Goes Again." Unknown source: "Chained to the Wall" / "Ages of You" / "Laughing" / "Just a Touch" / "Radio Free Europe" / "White Tornado"

Fables of R.E.M.
7" four-song EP taken from Nottingham, England, 11/21/84: "Pretty Persuasion" / "Radio Free Europe" / "West of the Fields" / "Rockville"

Finest Worksongs
Document and *Green* demos
1 LP: "Finest Worksong" / "Welcome to the Occupation" / "Exhuming McCarthy" / "Disturbance at the Heron House" / "Pop Song '89" / "End of the World" / "Fireplace" / "Lightnin' Hopkins" / "I

Remember California" / "Oddfellows Local 151" / "Get Up"/"You Are the Everything"

The Georgia Peaches
St. Petersburg, FL, 11/26/85
2 LP (Some copies on pink vinyl): "Feeling Gravity Pull" / "Harborcoat" / "Driver 8" / "Pilgrimage" / "Green Grow the Rushes" / "Maps and Legends" / "So. Central Rain" / "Laughing" / "Seven Chinese Brothers" "R's a Restless World" / "Can't Get There From Here" / "West of the Fields" / "Old Man Kensey" / "Auctioneer" / "Pretty Persuasion" / "Little America" / "Second Guessing" / "Shaking Through" / "Rock and Roll Star" (w/ Roger McGuinn) / "Toys in the Attic"

The Georgia Peaches—Ripe!
Tyrone's, Athens, GA, 1/10/81
2 LP: "Rave On" / "Burning Down" / "A Girl Like You" / "There She Goes Again" / "Pretty Persuasion" / "A Different Girl" / "Action" / "Narrator" / "Pretty Girl" / "Baby I" / "Permanent Vacation" / "Radio Free Europe" / "Sitting Still" / "Dangerous Times" / "I Don't Want You Anymore" / "Shaking Through" / "Little Girl" / "Rockville" / "Windout" / "Gardening at Night" / "Wait" / "Scherezade" / "Lisa Says" / "Mystery to Me" / "White Tornado"

Green in Concert
North American Tour, 1989
1 LP: "Be All You Can Be" / "Pop Song '89" / "Get Up" / "You Are the Everything" / "Stand" / "World Leader Pretend" / "The Wrong Child" / "Orange Crush" / "Turn You Inside Out" / "Hairshirt" / "I Remember California" / "Untitled" / "Army Theme Part 2"

I Don't Do Autographs
Various Live, 1987
Pittsburgh, PA: "Orange Crush" / "Stand" / "Turn Inside-Out" / "Pop Song '89." Unknown source: "Radio Free Europe" / "Sitting Still" / "Harborcoat"

It Crawled from the South
Peppermint Lounge, New York, 10/31/83

L.I.V.E.
University of Rochester
1 LP: "Harlem Nocturia" / "Moral Kiosk" / "Catapult" / "Pilgrimage" / "Return" / "Wolves, Lower" / "Talk About the Passion" / "Gardening at Night" / "Radio Free Europe"

Live in Chicago
Aragon Ballroom, Chicago, IL, 7/7/84 (picture disc and standard varieties): "Femme Fatale" / "Radio Free Europe" / "Gardening at Night" / "Sitting Still" / "9-9" "Windout" / "Driver 8" / "So. Central Rain" / "Harbor Coat" / "Hyena" / "Pretty Persuasion." Rock Influences (TV special): "Pale Blue Eyes" / "So You Want to Be a Rock and Roll Star" (w/ Roger McGuinn)

Mada Mada
Larry's Hideaway, Toronto, Canada, 7/9/88; City Gardens, Trenton, NY, 11/16/82
2 LP, Larry's Hideaway: "Laughing" / "Pilgrimage" / "There She Goes Again" / "Seven Chinese Brothers" / "Talk About the Passion" / "Sitting Still" / "Harborcoat" / "Catapult" / "Gardening at Night" / "9-9" / "Just a Touch" / "West of the Fields" / "Radio Free Europe" / "We Walk." Demos: "There She Goes Again" "Tighten Up" / "I Don't Want You Anymore." City Gardens: "Easy Come, Easy Go (Romance)" / "1,000,000" / "Pretty Persuasion" / "Ages of You" / "Pilgrimage" / "Wolves, Lower"

Mumble
Various Recordings, 1984–1986
1 LP, *Life's Rich Pageant* demo: "Underneath the Bunker" / "PSA" / "Cuyahoga." Nottingham, England, 11/26/84: "Gardening at Night" / "9-9" / "Auctioneer" "Windout" / "West of the Fields" / "Pretty Persuasion." Bayfront Center, St. Petersburg, IL, 11/26/85: "So. Central Rain" (acoustic) / "Swan Swan." Unknown source: "White Tornado"

Nottingham
Nottingham, England, 11/21/84
1 LP, included in *Finest Lunchbox*; released on green, clear, and red vinyl, as well as mixes of the above, covers released were green or red: "Hyena" / "Talk About Passion" / "Rockville" / "Auctioneer" / "So. Central Rain" / "Sitting Still" / "Old Man Kensey" / "9-9" / "Windout" / "Driver 8" / "Pretty Persuasion" / "Radio Free Europe" / "West of the Fields"

Pageantry
Universal Amphitheater, Los Angeles, CA, 9/30/86
2 LP (some copies on pink vinyl): "These Days" / "Radio Free Europe" / "Harborcoat" / "Sitting Still" / "The One I Love' Shaking Through" / "Feeling Gravity's Pull" / "Last Date" / "Driver 8" / "The Flowers of Guatemala" / "I Believe" / "Swan Swan H" / "Superman" / "Can't Get There from Here" / "Pretty Persuasion" / "Just a Touch" "Fall on Me" / "Cuyahoga" / "1,000,000" / "Strange" / "All Aboard" / "Life and How to Live It" / "Begin the Begin" / "So. Central Rain" (acoustic)

Pleasant Dreams
Music Hall, Seattle, WA, 6/27/84
2 LP: For set list, see *We're Blinking Just as Fast as We Can.*

The Pop Dream
Various covers
"Neverland" / "Gloria" / "There She Goes Again" / "California Dreamin' " / "Toy in the Attic" / "Paint It Black" / "I Can't Control Myself" / "Radar Love" / "So You Want to Be a Rock and Roll Star" / "I Can Only Give You What I Got" / "Secret Agent Man" / "See No Evil" / "Pills" / "Stepping Stone" / "Have You Ever Seen the Rain" / "Eight Miles High" / "Roadrunner" / "In the Year 2525" / "After Hours" / "God Save the

Queen" / "20th Century Boy" / "Smokin' in the Boys Room" / "Sweet Jane" / "Louis Louis" / "Pale Blue Eyes/Wild Thing" / "Chicken Train" / "Be Bop a Lula"

Pop Songs '89
Various Live, 1989
1 LP: "Pop Song '89" / "Get Up" / "You Are the Everything" / "King of Birds" / "World Leader Pretend" / "Orange Crush" / "Turn You Inside Out" / "Hairshirt" / "I Remember California" / "Rotary 10" / "11" / "Perfect Circle"

Pretty Pictures
Athens Rehearsals, 1980; Rhythmic Studios, San Francisco 9/11/83; *Chronic Town* demos; Reflection Studios, Charlotte, NC, 1988
2 LP, Athens, 1980: "That Best" / "All the Right Friends" / "Tighten Up" / "There She Goes Again" / "Moon River" / "That Beat" / "Burn It Down (Burning Down)." Rhythmic Studios: "All the Right Friends" / "Different Girl" / "Narrator" / "Just a Touch" / "Baby" "Mystery to Me" / "Permanent Vacation"

R=4
Various Live, 1985–1989
2 LP: "It's the End of the World as We Know It" / "Driver 8" / "Hard Luck Yosemite" / "Radio Free Europe" / "Stand" / "Orange Crush" / "Pop Song '89" / "The One I Love" / "Fall on Me" / "Smokin' in the Boys Room" / "Get Up" / "Hairshirt" / "Turn You Inside Out" / "Dark Globe" / "So You Want to Be a Rock and Roll Star" / "World Leader Pretend" / "Bandwagon" / "Finest Worksong" / "Wendell Gee" / "Strawberry Fields Forever" / "Femme Fatale" / "More This Than That"

Really Exciting Music
Chronic Town and *Reckoning* demos, etc.
1 LP, *Chronic Town* demos: "1,000,000" / "Ages of You" "Carnival of Sorts (Boxcars)" / "Shut Down (White Tornado)." Hip-Tone cuts: "Radio Free Europe" / "Sitting Still" / "There She Goes Again" (studio). *Reckoning* demos: "Windout" / "Pretty Persuasion" / "Time After Time" / "So. Central Rain" / "Little America"

Return of the Rickenbacker
Paradise Theater, Boston, MA, from WBCN-FM radio show, 7/13/83
1 LP: "Seven Chinese Brothers" / "Sitting Still" / "Pretty Persuasion" / "Harborcoat" / "West of the Fields" / "Radio Free Europe" / "Gloria" (from Tupelo's Tavern, New Orleans, 6/1/82) / "Ages of You" / "We Walk" / "1,000,000" / "There She Goes Again" / "California Dreaming" / "Carnival of Sorts (Boxcars)"

Rhythms et Melos
Music Hall, Seattle, WA, 6/27/84
1 LP: "Moral Kiosk" / "Driver 8" / "Catapult" / "Hyena" / "Pilgrimage" / "Old Man Kensey" / "Radio Free Europe" / "Little America"

Rolling Stone
Syrian Mosque, Pittsburgh, PA, 10/24/86
2 LP: "These Days" / "Harborcoat" / "Sitting Still" /
"The One I Love" / "West of the Fields" / "Shaking
Through" / "Feeling Gravity's Pull" / "White Tornado"
"The Flowers of Guatemala" / "Maps and Legends" /
"Driver 8" / "I Believe" / "Seven Chinese Brothers" /
"Superman" / "Can't Get There From Here" / "Pretty
Persuasion" / "Auctioneer (Another Engine)" / "Little
America" / "Fall on Me" / "Cuyahoga" / "1,000,000"

Smokin' in the Boys Room
Various Live and Studio, 1981–1983
1 LP, Drive-In Studio, 7/81: "White Tornado" / "Radio
Dub." Agora Ballroom, Hartford, CT, 7/20/89:
"Smokin' in the Boys Room." Larry's Hideaway,
Toronto, 7/83: "Moral Kiosk" / "Laughing" / "There
She Goes Again" / "Talk About the Passion" / "Sitting
Still" / "Harborcoat" / "9-9" / "West of the Fields" /
"Pretty Persuasion" / "Carnival of Sorts (Boxcars)"

So Much Younger Then
Tyrone's, Athens, GA, 1981
1 LP: "Body Count" / "A Different Girl" / "Action" /
"She's Such a Pretty Girl" / "Baby I" / "Permanent
Vacation" / "Wait" / "Scherezade" / "Lisa Says" /
"Mystery to Me" / "I Don't Want You Anymore" /
"Little Girl" / "Dangerous Times"

They Airbrushed This Box
Various acoustic, 1989. Packaged as five 7" 45s in a
boxed set, green vinyl: "Pop Song '89" / "Get Up" /
"Turn You Inside Out" / "You Are the Everything" /
"Stand" / "The Wrong Child" / "World Leader
Pretend" / "Orange Crush" / "Hairshirt" / "I Remember
California" / "Untitled" / "I Will Follow"

We Are Having a Heavenly Time
Page Auditorium, Duke University, Durham, NC,
9/26/84
1 LP: "Seven Chinese Brothers" / "Catapult" / "Radio
Free Europe" / "Letter Never Send" / "Khoetek" / "So.
Central Rain" / "Driver 8" / "Rockville" / "1,000,000" /
"Hyena" / "Old Man Kensey" / "Second Guessing"

We're Blinking Just as Fast as We Can
Music Hall, Seattle, WA, 6/27/84
2 LP: "Moral Kiosk" / "Catapult" / "Hyena" /
"Camera" "Pilgrimage" / "Talk About Passion" /
"Seven Chinese Brothers" / "So. Central Rain" / "Pretty
Persuasion" / "Gardening at Night" / "9-9" /
"Windout" / "Old Man Kensey" / "Radio Free Europe"
/ "Little America" / "Burning Down" / "Pale Blue
Eyes" / "1,000,000" / "So You Want to Be a Rock and
Roll Star" / "Carnival of Sorts (Boxcars)" / "Skank"

Working
Universal Amphitheater, Los Angeles, CA, 11/15/87
2 LP: "Finest Worksong" / "These Days" / "Welcome to
the Occupation" / "Pilgrimage" / "Disturbance at the
Heron House" / "Exhuming McCarthy" / "Don't Call

on Me (Orange Crush)" / " Feeling Gravity's Pull" /
"King of Birds" / "I Believe" / "Sitting Still" / "Ghost
Riders in the Sky" / "Pretty Persuasion" / "Superman" /
"Oddfellows Local 151" / "End of the World" / "Begin
the Begin" / "1,000,000" / "Wolves, Lower" / "See No
Evil" / "Pop Song '89" / "Ghost Riders" / "Cuyahoga" /
"Crazy."

Other titles include: *Contents* (Auckland, New Zealand),
The Eighties Do the Sixties (includes three R.E.M. cuts).

U.K. Interview Albums

R.E.M. interview disc
Baktabak bak 2057
Release date: September 1987
The material from this unauthorized picture disc comes
from a December 1984 BBC interview with Pete Buck
and a 1985 interview with all four members.

Rapid Mouth Movement
Powwow   POW01
Release date: September 1989

TOURS

1980:
Episcopal Church, Athens, GA	
(Their first-ever gig.)	4/5/80
Koffee Club, Athens, GA	4/19/80
Tyrone's, Athens, GA	5/5/80, 5/12/80
Memorial Hall, Athens, GA	5/15/80
Mad Hatter, GA	6/30/80
The Station, Carrboro, NC	7/18-19/80
Tyrone's, Athens, GA	10/4/80
Fox Theater, Atlanta, GA	12/6/80
Demos, Atlanta, GA	late 1980

1981:
Tyrone's, Athens, GA	1/10/81
Drive-In Studio, Winston-Salem, NC	3/5/81
Cantrell's, Nashville, TN	3/5/81
The Milestone, Charlotte, NC	3/28/81
Friday's, Greensboro, NC	3/31/81
New York New York, Augusta, GA	4/2/81
Vanderbilt, Nashville, TN	4/3/81
The Station, Carrboro, NC	4/4/81
The Pier, Raleigh, NC	4/6/81
Drive-In Studio, Winston-Salem, NC	4/15/81
The Ritz, New York, NY	6/16-17/81
Pilgrim Theater, New York, NY	9/16/81
Drive-In Studio, Winston-Salem, NC	10/2-4, 7/81
Viceroy Park, Charlotte, NC	11/7/81
First Avenue, Minneapolis, MN	11/26/81
Merlyns, Madison, WI	11/81
Tyrone's, Athens, GA	12/5/81

1982:
Maxwell's, Hoboken, NJ	1/30/82

RCA Demos, New York, NY	2/1-2/82
Danceteria, New York, NY	2/3-4/82
Beat Exchange, New Orleans, LA	3/12/82
Merlyn's, Madison, WI	4/24/82
First Avenue, Minneapolis, MN	4/26/82
Atlanta Arts Festival, Piedmont Park, Atlanta, GA	5/14/82
Drive-In Studio, NC	5/31/82
1+1 Club, Athens, GA	6/82
Toad's Place, New Haven, CT	6/10/82
Stand Cabaret, Marietta, GA	7/2/82
The Agora Club, Miami, FL	7/12/82
Music Machine, Los Angeles, CA	8/19/82
Old Waldorf, San Francisco, CA	8/24/82
First Avenue, Minneapolis, MN	9/22/82
Huff Gym, Champaign, IL	9/24/82
Marble Bar, Baltimore, MD	10/9/82
The Pier, Raleigh, NC	10/10/82
Maxwell's, Hoboken, NJ	10/28/82
Georgia Technical College, Atlanta, GA	10/31/82
The Bayou, Baton Rouge, LA	11/5/82
Tupelo's Tavern, Los Angeles, CA	11/6/82
WUTL, New Orleans, CA	11/6/82
City Gardens, Trenton, NJ	11/16/82
WUTK, Knoxville, TN	11/19/82
Hobo's, Knoxville, TN	11/19/82
Nashville, TN	11/20/82
Illinois	11/22/82
Nassau Coliseum, Uniondale, NY	11/24/82
Peppermint Lounge, New York, NY	11/25/82
The Agora Club, Miami, FL	12/7/82

1983:

Reflection Studios, Charlotte, NC	1/83
9:30 Club, Washington, DC	3/18/83
Page Auditorium, Duke University, Durham, NC	3/26/83
Memorial Hall, University of NC, Chapel Hill, NC	3/27/83
University of Miami, Coral Gables, FL	3/31/83
Palestra University, Rochester, NY	4/18/82
Spize, New York, NY	4/26/83
The Ritz, New York, NY	4/30/83
The Pier, Raleigh, NC	5/3/83
PB Scott's Music Hall, Blowing Rock, NC	5/4/83
Navy Island, St. Paul, MN	5/21/83
Headliners, Madison, WI	5/25/83
Red Rocks Amphitheatre, Morrison, CO	6/1/83
Old Waldorf, San Francisco, CA	6/14/83
Keystome, Berkeley, CA	6/20/83
The Blue Note, Columbia, MO	6/28/83
St. Andrews Hall, Detroit, MI	7/8/83
Larry's Hideaway, Toronto, Canada	7/9/83
Paradise Theater, Boston, MA	7/17/83
Toad's Place, New Haven, CT	7/17/83
Ripley's, Philadelphia, PA	7/20/83
Shea Stadium, Queens, NY	8/18/83
JFK Stadium, Philadelphia, PA	8/20/83
Capitol Centre, Largo, MD	8/21/83
Legion Field, Athens, GA	10/3/83
The Good Knight Pub, Piscataway, NJ	10/9/8

New York, NY	10/12/83
Providence, RI	10/13/83
Orono, ME	10/14/83
Colby College, Waterville, ME	10/15/83
Drumlins, Syracuse, NY	10/15/83
Queens College, Queens, NY	10/21/83
Peppermint Lounge, New York, NY	10/31/83
Late Night with David Letterman, New York, NY	10/83
Rhythmic Studio, San Francisco, CA	11/9/83
Kabuki Theatre, San Francisco, CA	11/10/83
Beverly Theatre, Los Angeles, CA	11/11/83
Montezuma Hall, SDSU Campus, San Diego, CA	11/12/83
The Tube (TV show), Newcastle, England	11/18/83
Dingwalls, Camden, London, England	11/19/83
The Marquee, London, England	11/22/83
The Paridiso, Amsterdam, Netherlands	11/23/83
Les Bains, Douches, Paris, France	11/24/83
Exo-7, Rouen, France	11/25/83
St. Petersburg, FL	11/28/83
Nickleodeon TV show	1983
Tyrone's, Athens, GA	1983

1984:

Reflections Sound Studio, Charlotte, NC	1/10-16/84
Harvard University, Cambridge, MA	3/23/84
The Paradiso, Amsterdam, Netherlands	4/8/84
Dan Effenaar, Eindhoven, Netherlands	4/10/84
Exo-7, Rouen, France	4/17/84
Eldorado, Paris, France	4/20/84
The Tin Can Club, Birmingham, England	4/24/84
The Gallery, Manchester, England	4/25/84
Warehouse, Leeds, England	4/26/84
Carioca Club, Worthing, England	4/29/84
The Marquee, London, England	4/30/84, 5/1/84
Saturday Live, BBC Radio, U.K.	5/5/84
Capitol Theater, Passaic, NJ	6/9/84
WLIR-FM radio broadcast	6/13/84
The Catalyst, Santa Cruz, CA	6/17/84
Mission Theatre, Santa Barbara, CA	6/18/84
Rock of the '80s (cable TV show), Palace Theater, Hollywood, CA	6/19/84
Delmar Fairgrounds, San Diego, CA	6/20/84
Warfield Theater, San Francisco, CA	6/22/84
Mountain Air Festival	6/23-24/84
Music Hall, Seattle, WA	6/27/84
Mardi Gras, Boise, ID	6/30/84
Rainbow Music Hall, Denver, CO	7/3/84
Orpheum Theater, Minneapolis, MN	7/5/84
Entertainment Tonight (TV show)	7/6/84
Summerfest Rockstage, Milwaukee, WI	7/6/84
Aragon Ballroom, Chicago, IL	7/7/84
Royal Oak Theater, Detroit, MI	7/8/84
Minett Hall, Rochester, NY	7/11/84
Salty Dog Saloon, Buffalo, NY	7/15/84
The Playpen, Wildwood, NJ	7/16/84
The Orpheum, Boston, MA	7/19/84
WBCN-FM, Boston, MA	7/19/84
The Agora, Hartford, CT	7/20/84
Beacon Theater, New York, NY	7/21-22/84

War Memorial Auditorium, Greensboro, NC	7/27/84
Fox Theatre, Atlanta, GA	7/28/84
IRS Cutting Edge (TV broadcast)	7/29/84
Pomona Valley Auditorium, Pomona, CA	9/5/84
Greek Theater, Los Angeles, CA	9/6/84
Palace West, Phoenix, AZ	9/8/84
Macky Auditorium, University of Colorado,	
Boulder, CO	9/11/84
Park Center, Charlotte, NC	9/23/84
Page Auditorium, Duke University,	
Durham, NC	9/25-26/84
University of S. Florida, Tampa, FL	9/28/84
Boca Raton, FL	9/29/84
Gainsville, FL	9/30/84
McAllister Auditorium, New Orleans, LA	10/2/84
Oxford, MS	10/3/84
Carbondale, IL	10/5/84
Graham Chapel, St. Louis, MO	10/6/84
Dekalb, IL	10/7/84
Hill Auditorium, Ann Arbor, MI	10/8/84
Charlottesville, VA	10/11/84
University of Bridgeport, Bridgeport, CT	10/13/84
Fine Arts Center, Amherst, MA	10/15/84
WMUA-FM (radio broadcast), Amherst, MA	10/15/84
Veterans Memorial Auditorium,	
Providence, Rhode Island	10/16/84
Tower Theater, Philadelphia, PA	10/17/84
Rehearsal Hall, Tokyo, Japan	11/4/84
Waseda University, Tokyo, Japan	11/5/84
Music School Auditorium, Japan	11/8/84
College gig near Tokyo, Japan	11/10/84
Gymnasium near Tokyo, Japan	11/11/84
The Circus, Oslo, Norway	11/13/84
Tiffany's, Newcastle, England	11/15/84
Manchester Polytechnic, Manchester, England	11/17/84
Picadilly Radio, Manchester, England	11/17/84
Royal Court, Liverpool, England	11/18/84
Old Grey Whistle Test, London, England	11/20/84
Rock City, Nottingham, England	11/21/84
University of East Anglia, Norwich, England	11/23/84
University of Essex, Colchester, England	11/24/84
Birmingham University,	
Birmingham, England	11/26/84
Keisas, Leicester, England	11/27/84
New Ocean Club, Cardiff, Wales	11/28/84
Queensway Hall, Dunstable, England	11/29/84
The Lyceum, London, England	12/2/84
SFX Centre, Dublin, Ireland	12/4/84
Civic Center, Atlanta, GA	12/31/84

1985:

Athens, GA	4/22/85
Bucknell University, Lewisburg, PA	4/25/85
Suny, Binghampton, NJ	4/26/85
Brown University, Providence, RI	4/27/85
Rutgers University, Piscataway, NJ	4/28/85
Drew University, Madison, NJ	4/30/85
New Athletic Center, MIT, Cambridge, MA	4/30/85
Lansing Arena, Williamstown, MA	5/4/85
Alumni Arena, University of Buffalo,	
Buffalo, NY	5/5/85

McGaw Hall, Northwestern University,	
Chicago, IL	5/8/85
Iowa City, IA	5/9/85
Richmond, VA	5/12/85
Stock Pavillion, Madison, WI	5/15/85
Meredith College Amphitheater,	
Raleigh, NC	5/27/85
Drew University, Madison, NJ	5/30/85
Milton Keynes Bowl, England	6/22/85
Piccadily Radio, Manchester, England	6/23/85
Manchester International,	
Manchester, England	6/24/85
Coasters, Edinburgh, Scotland,	6/25/85
Tiffany's, Newcastle, England	6/26/85
Warwick University, Coventry, England	6/27/85
Capitol Radio, London, England	6/28/85
Slane Castle, Dublin, Ireland	6/29/85
Piccadily Radio, Manchester, England	6/30/85
Saturday Live (BBC FM radio interview)	7/6/85
Torhout Festival, Belgium	7/6/85
Werchter Festival, Belgium	7/7/85
Portland, OR	7/11/85
Paramount Theatre, Seattle, WA	7/12/85
Commodore Ballroom, Vancouver, Canada	7/13/85
Cable TV, Vancouver, Canada	7/13/85
Edmonton, Alberta, Canada	7/15/85
Calgary, Alberta, Canada	7/16/85
WNYU-FM, New York, NY	7/18/85
Fresno, CA	7/19/85
Community Theater, Berkeley, CA	7/20/85
Rockline (radio interview), Hollywood, CA	7/22/85
Civic Auditorium, Santa Cruz, CA	7/23/85
Santa Barbara, CA	7/24/85
Open Air Theater, San Diego, CA	7/26/85
Greek Theater, Hollywood, CA	7/27/85
Irvine Meadows Ampitheater, Irvine, CA	7/28/85
Rock Today, WNEW-FM, New York, NY	7/29/85
Palace West, Phoenix, AZ	7/29/85
San Antonio, TX	7/31/85
Austin, TX	8/1/85
Cullen Auditorium, Houston, TX	8/2/85
Dallas, TX	8/3/85
Minneapolis, MN	8/5/85
Civic Center Forum, St. Paul, MN	8/6/85
U.I.C. Pavilion, Chicago, IL	8/7/85
State Theater, Kalamazoo, MI	8/9/85
Fox Theater, Detroit, MI	8/10/85
Cleveland, OH	8/12/85
Syria Mosque, Pittsburg, PA	8/13/85
Auditorium Theater, Rochester, NY	8/15/85
Concert Hall, Toronto, Canada	8/16/85
Much Music (TV interview), Toronto, Canada	8/16/85
New Music (TV interview), Toronto, Canada	8/16/85
Barrymore's, Ottawa, Canada	8/17/85
Montreal, Canada	8/18/85
Cumberland County Civic Center,	
Portland, OR	8/20/85
Walter Brown Arena, Boston, MA	8/21/85
Leroy Theatre, Pawtucket, RI	8/23/85
The Agora, Hartford, CT	8/24/85
J.B. Scott's, Albany, NY	8/25/85

Baltimore, MD	8/26/85
Tower Theater, Philadelphia, PA	8/28/85
Washington, D.C.	8/29/85
Capitol Theater, Passaic, PA	8/30/85
Radio City Music Hall, New York, NY	8/31/85
"Rock Today" (radio interview), WNEW-FM,	
New York, NY	9/2/85
The Paradiso, Amsterdam, Netherlands	10/1/85
Zeche, Bochum, Germany	10/2/85
Arena, Rotterdam, Netherlands	10/3/85
Vooruit, Gent, Belgium	10/5/85
Frankfurt, Germany	10/6/85
Alabamahalle, Munich, German	10/7/85
Berlin, Germany	10/9/85
Markthalle, Hamburg, Germany	10/10/85
Cologne, Germany	10/11/85
Uni Aula, Saarbrücken, Germany	10/13/85
Eldorado, Paris, France	10/14/85
Salle Maliere, Lyon, France	10/15/85
Geneva, Switzerland	10/16/85
Mannheim, West Germany	10/18/85
Piccadilly Radio, Manchester, England	
(FM radio interview)	10/20/85
The Ritz, Manchester, England	10/20/85
The Roxy, Nottingham, England	10/21/85
Octagon Centre, Sheffield, England	10/22/85
Barrowlands, Glasgow, Scotland	10/23/85
The Tube (TV show), Newcastle, England	10/25/85
Royal Court, Liverpool, England	10/26/85
Hammersmith Palais, London, England	10/27/85
Hammersmith Palais, London, England	10/28/85
CU Events Center, Boulder, CO	
(start of "Reconstruction III" tour)	11/2/85
Arts & Science Auditorium, Laramie, WY	11/3/85
Omaha, NE	11/5/85
Kansas City, MO	11/6/85
University of Indiana, Bloomington, IN	11/8/85
CMJ Awards show, Beacon Theater, NY	11/9/85
Lexington, KY	11/11/85
Nashville, TN	11/12/85
Memphis, TN	11/13/85
Ames, IA	11/15/85
Radio Sheffield, Sheffield, England	
(FM radio interview with Peter Buck)	11/15/85
Champaign, IL	11/16/85
Kiel Opera House, St. Louis, MO	11/17/85
New Orleans, Los Angeles, CA	11/19/85
Tuscaloosa, AL	11/21/85
Tallahassee, FL	11/22/85
Jacksonville, FL	11/23/85
James L. Knight Center, Miami, FL	11/24/85
Bayfront Theater, St. Petersburg, FL	11/26/85
Civic Center, Savannah, GA	11/27/85
Fox Theater, Atlanta, GA	11/29-30/85
Civic Center, Raleigh, NC	12/2/85
Boone, NC	12/3/85
Chrysler Auditorium, Norfolk, VA	12/4/85
The Mosque, Richmond, VA	12/5/85
Washington & Lee University,	
Lexington, VA	12/6/85
Reynolds Auditorium, Winston-Salem, NC	12/8/85

Veterans Memorial Auditorium,	
Columbus, OH	12/10/85
Columbia, SC	12/11/85
Park Center, Charlotte, NC	12/13/85
The World, New York, NY	12/20/85
1986:	
The Ritz, New York, NY	1/9/86
40 Watt Club, Athens, GA	1/20/86
Athens, GA	3/8/86
WLIR-FM/WNYU-FM/K-ROCK	
(radio interviews) New York, NY	8/19/86
WLUP-FM (radio interview),	
Chicago, IL	8/20/86
Oak Mountain Amphitheater,	
Birmingham, AL	9/5/86
University of Indiana, Bloomington, IN	9/6/86
"Rock Today" (radio interview), WNEW-FM,	
New York, NY	9/6/86
Taft Theater, Cincinnati, OH	9/7/86
Memorial Auditorium, Louisville, KY	9/8/86
Grand Ole Opry, Nashville, TN	9/10/86
Municipal Auditorium, Jackson, MS	9/11/86
Saenger Theatre, New Orleans	9/12/86
Mudd Island Amphitheatre, Memphis, TN	9/13/86
Robinson Auditorium, Little Rock, AR	9/15/86
Music Hall, Oklahoma City, OK	9/17/86
The Coliseum, Austin, TX	9/18/86
Southern Star Amphitheater, Houston, TX	9/19/86
The Bandshell, Dallas State Fairgrounds,	
Dallas, TX	9/20/86
Pan American Center, Las Cruces, NM	9/22/86
Mesa Amphitheater, Mesa, AZ	9/23/86
Pacific Amphitheater, Cosa Mesa, CA	9/24/86
Greek Theater, Berkeley, CA	9/26/86
County Bowl, Santa Barbara, CA	9/27/86
UCSD Gym, San Diego, CA	9/28/86
Universal Amphitheater, Los Angeles, CA	9/30/86
Oakland Coliseum, Oakland, CA	10/1/86
Holt Centre, Eugene, OR	10/2/86
Civic Auditorium, Portland, OR	10/3/86
Paramount Theater, Seattle, WA	10/4/86
War Memorial Arena, BC, Canada	10/5/86
Fairgrounds Coliseum, Salt Lake City, UT	10/7/86
CU Events Center, Boulder, CO	10/9/86
Pershing Auditorium, Lincoln, NE	10/10/86
Memorial Hall, Kansas City, MO	10/11/86
Kiel Opera House, St. Louis, MO	10/12/86
Roy Wilkins Auditorium, St. Louis, MO	10/14/86
Honcher Auditorium, Iowa City, IO	10/15/86
Oriental Theater, Milwaukee, WI	10/17/86
Grand Center, Grand Rapids, MI	10/18/86
UIC Pavillion, University of Illinois,	
Chicago, IL	10/19/86
Chick Evans Fieldhouse, Dekalb, IL	10/21/86
Fox Theater, Detroit, MI	10/22/86
Public Hall, Cleveland, OH	10/23/86
Syria Mosque, Pittsburgh, PA	10/24/86
Shea's Theater, Buffalo, NY	10/26/86
Massey Hall, Toronto, Canada	10/27/86
Montreal, Canada	10/29/86

University of New Hampshire Fieldhouse, Durham, NH	10/30/86
UVM Patrick Gym, Burlington, VT	10/31/86
Wang Centre, Boston, MA	11/2/86
Felt Forum, New York, NY	11/6-7/86
The Coliseum, New Haven, CT	11/8/86
Spectrum Showcase, Philadelphia, PA	11/9/86
Charlottesville, VA	11/11/86
Washington, DC	11/12/86
William & Mary Hall, Williamsburg, VA	11/14/86
Cameron Indoor Stadium, Duke University, Durham, NC	11/15/86
Wilmington, NC	11/16/86
Township Hall, Columbia, SC	11/17/86
Georgia Southern College, Statesboro, GA	11/19/86
Civic Auditorium, Jacksonville, FL	11/20/86
St. Petersburg, FL	11/21/86
James L. Knight Centre, Miami, FL	11/22/86
Fox Theatre, Atlanta, GA	11/24-26/86

1987:

Uptown Lounge, Athens, GA	3/25/87
McCabe's Guitar Shop, Santa Monica, CA	5/24/87
Hammersmith Odeon, London, England	9/12/87
Muziekcentrum, Utrecht, Netherlands	9/14/87
Knoxville, TN	10/1/87
Clemson University, Clemson, SC	10/2/87
Durham, NC	10/3-4/87
New York, NY	10/6/87
Radio City Music Hall, New York, NY	10/7/87
William & Mary Hall, Williamsburg, VA	10/9/87
Patriot Centre, Fairfax, VA	10/10/87
State College, PA	10/11/87
UVA, Charlottesville, VA	10/12/87
Charleston, WV	10/14/87
Philadelphia, PA	10/16/87
New Haven, CT	10/17/87
Worcester, MA	10/18/87
Providence, RI	10/19/87
Pittsburgh, PA	10/23/87
Columbus, OH	10/24/87
East Lansing, MI	10/26/87
Lafayette, IN	10/27/87
Ann Arbor, MI	10/29/87
Madison, WI	11/3/87
University of Chicago Pavilion, IL	11/4-5/87
Champaign, IL	11/7/87
Kansas City, MO	11/8/87
Lincoln, NE	11/9/87
St. Louis, MO	11/10/87
Los Angeles, CA	11/11/87
Oakland, CA	11/13/87
Holt Center, Irving, CA	11/14/87
Universal Amphitheater, Los Angeles, CA	11/15/87
Tempe, AZ	11/16/87
Dallas, TX	11/18/87
Austin, TX	11/19/87
Houston, TX	11/20/87
Oxford, MS	11/22/87
Auburn, AL	11/23/87

Atlanta, GA	11/24-25/87
Atlanta, GA	11/28/87

1989:

MZA Stadium, Tokyo, Japan	1/26-27/89
Town Hall, Christchurch, New Zealand	2/2-3/89
Logan Campbell Centre, Auckland, New Zealand	2/4/89
Concert Hall, Perth, Australia	2/8-9/89
The Barton Theatre, Adelaide, Australia	2/11/89
Festival Hall, Melbourne, Australia	2/12/89
Festival Hall, Brisbane, Australia	2/15/89
Hordern Pavillion, Sydney, Australia	2/17/89
Louisville, KY	3/1/89
Carbondale, IL	3/2/89
St. Louis, MO	3/3/89
Chicago, IL	3/4/89
Iowa City, IA	3/7/89
Minneapolis, MN	3/8/89
Omaha, NE	3/10/89
Argo Arena, Sacramento, CA	3/13/89
Oakland Coliseum, Oakland, CA	3/14/89
The Forum, Los Angeles, CA	3/15/89
Sports Arena, San Diego, CA	3/16/89
ASU Activities Center, Tempe, AZ	3/18/89
San Antonio, TX	3/20/89
Austin, TX	3/21/89
Dallas, TX	3/22/89
Houston, TX	3/23/89
Shreveport, Los Angeles, CA	3/25/89
New Orleans, Los Angeles, CA	3/27/89
Birmingham, AL	3/28/89
Memphis, TN	3/30/89
Murphreesboro, TN	3/30/89
Atlanta, GA	4/1-2/89
Cincinatti, OH	4/4/89
3 Coliseum	4/6/89
The Coliseum, Morganfield, WV	4/7/89
The Centrum, Worcester, MA	4/9/89
Madison Square Garden, New York, NY	4/10/89
War Memorial Auditorium, Syracuse, NY	4/11/89
Maple Leaf Gardens, Toronto, Canada	4/12/89
Montreal Forum, Montreal, Canada	4/14/89
Civic Center, Portland, ME	4/15/89
Boston Garden, Boston, MA	4/16/89
Capitol Center, MD	4/18/89
The Spectrum, Philadelphia, PA	4/20/89
Richfield Coliseum, VA	4/21/89
Dean Smith Center, Chapel Hill, NC	4/22/89
The Coliseum, Charlotte, NC	4/23/89
Carolina Coliseum, Columbia, SC	4/25/89
Civic Center, Savannah, GA	4/26/89
The Sun Dome, Tampa, FL	4/28/89
Miami Arena, Miami, FL	4/29/89
Orlando Arena, Orlando, FL	4/30/89
Leon County Civic Center, Tallahassee, FL	5/2/89
Von Braun Arena, Huntsville, AL	5/3/89
Dusseldorf, Germany	5/9/89
Munich, Germany	5/9/89
Bieldfeld, Germany	5/12/89
Frankfurt, Germany	5/13/89

Hamburg, Germany	5/14/89
Pink Pop Festival, Netherlands	5/15/89
De Montfort Hall, Leicester, England	5/17/89
Newport, Gwent, Wales	5/18/89
Guild Hall, Portsmouth, England	5/19/89
Royal Court, Liverpool, England	5/21/89
Concert Hall, Nottingham, England	5/22/89
Edinburgh, Scotland	5/23/89
Glasgow, Scotland	5/24/89
Newcastle, England	5/26/89
Manchester, England	5/27/89
Hammersmith Odeon, London, England	5/28, 30/89
NEC, Birmingham, England	5/31/89
Palasport, Bologna, Italy	6/16/89
Palatrussardi, Milano, Italy	6/17/89
Wembley Arena, London, England	6/22/89
Provinssirock, Finland	6/4/89
Saga, Copenhagen, Denmark	6/6/89
Saturday Sequence, BBC Radio 1, England	6/10/89
Zurich, Switzerland	6/14/89
Rock Torhout Festival, Belgium	7/1/89
Rock Werchter Festival, Belgium	7/2/89
Market Square, Indianapolis, IN	9/8/89
Pine Knob, Clarkston, MI	9/9/89
Civic Center, Pittsburgh, PA	9/10/89
Great Woods, Mansfield, MA	9/15-16/89
Mann Music Center, Philadelphia, PA	9/17/89
Meadowlands, East Rutherford, NJ	9/19/89
Nassau Coliseum, Uniondale, NY	9/20/89
Merriweather Post, Columbia, MD	9/22-23/89
University of Dayton, Dayton, OH	9/26/89
Assembly Hall, Champaign, IL	9/27/89
Notre Dame, South Bend, IN	9/29/89
Alpine Valley, East Troy, WI	9/30/89
Hilton Coliseum, Ames, IO	10/1/89
Devaney Sports Center, Lincoln, NE	10/3/89
McNichols Sports Arena, Denver, CO	10/5/89
Salt Palace, Salt Lake City, UT	10/7/89
University Center, Boise, ID	10/9/89
Washington State Coliseum, Pullman, WA	10/10/89
Coliseum, Seattle, WA	10/11/89
Coliseum, Portland, OR	10/13/89
Pacific National Exhibition, Vancouver, Canada	10/14/89
Pacific Amphitheater, Costa Mesa, CA	10/18/89
Pavilion, Concord, CA	10/20/89
Shoreline Amphitheater, Mountain View, CA	10/21/89
Compton Terrace, Phoenix, AZ	10/24/89
Community Centre Arena, Tuscon, AZ	10/25/89
Pan Am Centre, Las Cruces, NM	10/26/89
Myriad Arena, Oklahoma City, OK	10/28/89
Louisiana State Assembly, Baton Rouge, LA	10/30/89
Leon County Arena, Tallahassee, FL	11/1/89
University of Tennessee Arena, TN	11/3/89
Thompson Boling Arena, Chattanooga, TN	11/4/89
Rupp Arena, Lexington, KY	11/5/89
Civic Center, Roanoke, VA	11/7/89
Hampton Coliseum, Hampton, VA	11/8/89
Coliseum, Greensboro, NC	11/10/89
Coliseum, Macon, GA	11/11/89

1990:	
40 Watt Club, Athens, GA	4/5/90
40 Watt Club, Athens, GA	7/31/90
1991:	
BBC Radio 1, London, England	3/13/91
The Late Show, BBC-TV, London, England	3/14/91
The Borderline, London, England	3/14-15/91
Shocking Club, Milan, Italy	3/22/91
Snap, KCRW-FM, Los Angeles, CA	4/3/91
Mountain Stage	5/11/91
40 Watt Club, Athens, GA	6/15/91

SESSIONS AND GUEST APPEARANCES

Peter Buck

Robyn Hitchcock and Peter Buck:
"Flesh No. 1" (demo version 7" flexidisc)
  Bucketful of Brains BOB.17   UK 87
Robyn Hitchcock (Buck on guitar):
Globe of Frogs   (LP)
  A&M AMA 5182 UK 88
  A&M SP 5182 US 88
  songs: "Chinese Bones," "Flesh Number One"
Balloon Man (promo 12")
  A&M SP-17530 US 88
  song:"Globe of Frogs"
Queen Elvis
  (LP)   A&M 5241 US 89
  (CD)   A&M CD 5241 US 89
  songs: "Madonna of the Wasps," "Wax
  Doll," "Swirling," "Freeze"
"Madonna of the Wasps" / "One Long Pair
  of Eyes" (acoustic) / "More Than This"
  (promo CD only)
  A&M CD 17718 US 89
Played live together Athens, GA, 3/25/88, live recording broadcast
Nigel & the Crosses (including Hitchcock and Buck)
Time Between—A Tribute to the Byrds (LP/CD)
  Imaginary ILL CD400 UK 89
  song: "Wild Mountain Thyme"
"Wild Mountain Thyme" (DJ-only 7")
  (white label) US 89
"The Queen of Eyes" / "Purple Haze" (live 7")
  Bucketful of Brains BOB.28 UK 90
Replacements
Let It Be   (LP)
  Zippo ZONG 002 UK 84
Let It Be (LP)
  Twin Tone TTR 8441 US 84
"I Will Dare" (12")
  Twin Tone TTR 8440 US 84
Dream Academy
Dream Academy (LP)
  Warner Brothers 25265 US 85
  Blanco y Negro UK 85

song: "The Party"
The Fleshtones
Speed Connection II (live LP)
   IRS 5627 US 85
   IRS ILP 26412 UK 85
   songs: "When the Night Falls," "Wind Out"
Dreams So Real (produced by Buck)
"Everywhere Girl" / "Whirl" (7")
   Coyote TTC 8556 US 85
   Coyote TTC 8688 US 86
Woofing Cookies (produced by Buck)
"In the City" / "VB Side" (7")
   Midnight MID4512 US 86
   song: "In the City"
Hanging Out at Midnight (compilation LP)
   Midnight MIRLP 127 US 86
   song: "Girl Next Door"
The Feelies (coproduced by Buck)
The Good Earth   (LP)
   Coyote TTC 8673 US 86
No One Knows (12" EP)
   Coyote 8695 US 86
   Rough Trade RTT 180 UK 86
The Fulltime Men (guitar, banjo; coproduced by Buck)
"I Got Wheels" / "One More Time" /"Way Down
South" (12")
   Coyote TTC 8562 US 86
What Goes On
   UK 86
Your Face, My Fist (LP)
   Coyote TTC 88138 US 88
   songs: "I Got Wheels," "High on Drugs"
The Upbeats (Buck plays guitar on)
Pop Songs (LP)
   Laser LLP 102 US 86
   song: "Just Another Pop Song"
Bruce Joyner (Buck plays guitar)
Hot Georgia Nights (LP)
   New Rose ROSE 129 FR 87
   songs: "The World Needs a Little More Love,"
      "Melrose Avenue"
Charlie Picket & the MC3 (Buck produced album;
plays on)
In the Wilderness (LP)
   Fundamental Music SAVE066 UK 88
   Safety Net US 88
   songs: "Death Leather," "John the Revelator"
Tommy Keene (Buck plays guitar, mandolin)
Based on Happy Times (LP)
   Geffen 759924221 US 89
   songs: "Our Car Club," "A Way Out"
Drivin-N-Cryin (plays dulcimer)
Mystery Road (LP)
   Island 91226 US 89
Kevin Kinney (produced)
MacDougal Blues (LP/CD)
   Island 791331-1/2 US 90
Peter Buck & Nikki Sudden (coproduced; played)
"Sun Is Shining" (7" flexi)
   Reflex magazine (Fall) US 90
Run Westy Run (coproduced)

Green Cat Island   (LP)
   Twin Tone TTR89199-1 US 90

Michael Stipe

Tanzplagen (Stipe's noise band)
Live demo (cassette)
   no label US 81/82
Jason & the Scorchers
Fervor (mini-LP)
   Praxis PR 6654 US 83
   EMI America SQ 19008 US 84
   songs: "Hot Nights in Georgia"
   (sings harmony, cowrote...)
   "Both Sides of the Line" (sings harmony)
Golden Palominos
"Omaha" / "I.D. (Like a Version)" (7")
   Celluloid SCEL 56 (sings lead on A sides) US 85
"Omaha" / "For a Few Dollars More" (12")
   CEL 183 US 85
   (sings leads)
Visions of Excess   (LP)
   Celluloid CEll6118 US 85
   songs: "Boy (Go)" (cowrote), "Clustering Train,"
   "Omaha"
Trilogy (triple-LP compilation)
   Celluloid CELL 80808 US 85
   songs: "Omaha," "Clustering Train"
Community Trolls *Don't Shoot* (advance promo
cassette only)
   Zippo ZONG 009 UK 86
   song: "Tainted Obligations"
OFB (Our Favorite Band)
Saturday Nights...Sunday Mornings (LP)
   Praxis/BT6041-1-B US 87
   song: "Dreamin' of Eternity"
Hugo Largo
(coproduced most and contributed musically to)
Drum (LP)
   Relativity 88561-8167-1 US 87
10,000 Maniacs
In My Tribe (LP)
   Elektra 960738 US 87
   song: "A Campfire Song" (duet)
Hetch Hetchy (produced)
Make Djibouti (mini-LP)
   Texas Hotel 7 US 88
Various Artists (sings on...)
Stay Awake (LP)
   A&M SP3918 US/UK1988
   song: "Little April Shower"
Syd Straw (cowrote and duets on)
Surprise (LP)
   Virgin 91266 US 89
   song: "Future 40's (String of Pearls)"
"Future 40's (String of Pearls)" (7")
   Virgin VUST 6   US1989
Vic Chestnutt (produced)
Little (LP/CD)
   Texas Hotel 20/20CD US 89
Chicksaw Mudd Puppies (coproduced)

White Dirt (mini-LP)
  Texas Hotel 843 2171 US 90
  (Stipe has also worked on...Coffee Country 8-Track,
  not yet released.)

Mike Mills

Kilkenny Cats
Hands Down (LP)
  Coyote TTC 8670 US 86
  (produced by Mike Mills)
Waxing Poetics
Hermitage (LP)
  Emergo EM 9610 US 88
  (produced by Mike Mills)
Billy James
Sixes & Sevens (LP)
  Twilight Records TR016 US 88
  (produced by Mike Mills)

Peter Buck

Kevin Kinney
MacDougal Blues (LP/CD)
  Island 7.91331-1/2 US 90
  (produced by Peter Buck)

Bill Berry

Michelle Malone
New Experience (LP)
  Illuminous June US 88
  (Bill Berry plays drums on the track "Into the
  Night.")
Thirteen-One-Eleven
"My Bible Is the Latest TV Guide / Things I'd Like To
  Say" (12")
Dog Gone DOG 13111 USA 1990
  (solo single.)

Collaborations Involving Multiple Members of R.E.M.

The Spongetones
Torn Apart (mini-LP)
  Pipete 2154 US 84
  (hand claps on "Shock Therapy")
Hindu Love Gods
"Gonna Have a Good Time Tonight / Narrator" (7")

IRS IRS-52867 US 86
  (white label)
Hindu Love Gods (LP/CD)
  Giant 24406-1/-2 US 90
  (Single features: Mike Mills, Bill Berry, and Peter
  Buck, together with Bryan Cook and Warren Zevon.
  The full Hindu Love Gods album features the three
  R.E.M.-sters mentioned above.)
Warren Zevon
Sentimental Hygiene (LP)
  Virgin 7.90603-1 US 87
"Sentimental Hygiene" (7")
  Virgin VS 995 US 87
  (Peter Buck, Bill Berry, and Mike Mills provide
  instrumentation on most of the LP; Michael Stipe
  contributes harmony vocals on "Bad Karma." Berry,
  Buck, and Mills cowrote "Even a Dog Can Shake
  Hands" with Zevon.)
Indigo Girls
Indigo Girls (LP)
  Epic 45044 US 89
Indigo Girls (LP)
  CBS 4634911 UK 89
  (Michael Stipe sings backing vocals on the track "Kid
  Fears"; Peter Buck, Mike Mills, and Bill Berry all play
  on "Tried to Be True.")
Robyn Hitchcock and the Egyptians
Perspex Island (LP/CD)
  A&M 7502-15368-1/2 US 91
  (Michael Stipe sings on "She Doesn't Exist." Peter
  Buck plays on "Lysander," "So You Think You're in
  Love," "Child of the Universe," "Earthly Paradise,"
  "Oceanside," "She Doesn't Exist," "Vegetation &
  Dimes," and "Ride.")
Nikki Sudden
"Belong to You" / "Alley of the Street" / "Jigsaw
  Blues"
  UFO 45003 CD UK 91
Peter Holsapple
"Big Black Truck" / "Death Garage" / "96 Second
  Blowout" (7")
  Car Records CRR 5 US978
Luxury Condos Coming to Your Neigborhood (LP)
  (Compilation. Holsapple appears as "Mr. Bonus" and
  performs "Elvis, What Happened?")
  Coyote TTC 8559 US 85
Live, Melbourne, 1989 (cassette only)
  Fast Fictions FAST .001 AU

- -

DEAR SENATOR:

I SUPPORT THE **MOTOR VOTER BILL**. ACCORDING TO THE U.S. CENSUS, IN THE LAST PRESIDENTIAL ELECTION, 78% OF 18-29 YEAR OLDS WHO WERE REGISTERED TO VOTE, VOTED. WE AREN'T AS APATHETIC AS SOME PEOPLE THINK. IT'S JUST THAT THE LAWS MAKE IT HARD FOR MANY OF US TO REGISTER.

I HOPE I CAN SAY MY SENATOR SUPPORTS THE **MOTOR VOTER BILL**.

YOUR CONSTITUENT,

_____
(NAME)

_____
(ADDRESS)

_____
(PHONE)

ROCK THE VOTE

DEPT. 171

P.O. BOX 64742

LOS ANGELES, CA.

90064